BULBS, CORMS
AND TUBERS

BULBS, CORMS AND TUBERS

Michael Joseph/Rainbird

First published in Great Britain in 1985
by Michael Joseph Ltd,
44 Bedford Square, London WC1 and
The Rainbird Publishing Group Ltd,
40 Park Street, London W1 who
designed and produced this book.

Contributors: Brian Carter, Alan Toogood

© 1985 The Rainbird Publishing Group Limited

Adapted from *The Complete Handbook of Garden Plants*
first published by Michael Joseph Ltd and
The Rainbird Publishing Group Ltd in 1984.

British Library Cataloguing in Publication Data
Bulbs, corms and tubers. —— (Garden guides)
  1. Bulbs   2. Corms   3. Tubers
  I. Series
635.9´44   SB425
ISBN 0-7181-2526-6

Text set by SX Composing Ltd, Rayleigh, Essex, England
Colour originated by Bridge Graphics Limited, Hull, England
Printed and bound by Mateu Cromo Artes Graficas, S.A.,
Madrid, Spain

Contents

Illustration Credits

Introduction

Bulbs, corms, tubers and rhizomes are storage organs which contain water and plant foods to tide plants over their dormant or resting period, or to enable plants to survive periods of drought. Most of these organs are produced near the soil surface, as with the swollen rhizomes of bearded irises; and the tops of some bulbs may protrude above the soil surface.

Bulbs A bulb, for example a daffodil or hyacinth, is composed of fleshy scales which are in fact modified leaves, and at the base is a compressed stem, rather plate-like in structure. The centre of the bulb contains an embryo shoot, and in flowering-size bulbs an embryo flower. Some bulbs are covered with a papery outer layer or 'tunic'.
Corms A corm is a thickened or swollen stem base, an example being the crocus. Again, most corms are enclosed in a papery tunic. During the growing period the original corm shrivels up and is replaced with a new one formed above it.
Tubers These are swollen stems or roots. A stem tuber, for example cyclamen and begonia, produces growth buds, while a root tuber, as in dahlias, does not produce buds, the new growth coming from a 'crown' above the tubers.
Rhizomes These are modified stems, and in the examples in this book are swollen for water and food storage. An example is the bearded iris. Rhizomes grow below or above the soil surface, rooting as they go and producing new shoots at the ends.

Bulbs, corms, tubers and rhizomes form an important group of garden plants and virtually every part of the ornamental garden can be planted with suitable kinds. Many gardeners will grow them in borders, with shrubs, perennials and other plants.

The rock garden makes an ideal home for many of the dwarf genera, like anemone, baboon flower, crocus, dwarf iris, grape hyacinth, wood sorrel and striped squill. Other kinds, such as belladonna lily and Mariposa lily love hot dry places. At the other extreme there are many subjects for dappled shade and moist soil – some of the anemones, snowdrop, arisaema, snow-flakes, camasses, cyclamen, bluebells and lilies.

Many of these are particularly attractive naturalized in grass – for short grass one would use, for example, crocus, snowdrop and the dwarf narcissus; while subjects able to cope with long grass include colchicums, lilies and the taller narcissus.

Bulbs are often planted in spring-bedding schemes, hyacinths and the hybrid tulips in particular. Often spring-bedded plants such as wallflowers, forget-me-nots, double-flowered daisies and polyanthus are mixed with them.

Some of the plants included here make excellent cut flowers – dahlias, gladioli, many of the irises, African corn lilies, lilies and Persian buttercups are just a few.

Soil preparation and planting

Thorough soil preparation is essential: dig deep, at least to the depth of the fork or spade. Treatment depends on the soil type, but it is safe to say that all bulbs, corms, tubers and rhizomes like well-drained conditions. Soils which lie very wet over winter are liable to result in the storage organs rotting. If the soil is heavy (such as clay) and poorly drained, copious amounts of grit, coarse sand or gravel should be worked in during digging, mixing it well into the soil. This will open up the soil and ensure better drainage. However, if soil is light (such as sands and chalky types) then some provision should be made to conserve soil moisture. Dig in organic material such as peat, leaf mould, pulverized bark or well-rotted garden compost. Dahlias like a very rich moist soil and one could not do better than incorporate well-rotted manure in the autumn before spring planting.

The times of planting vary enormously, as do the depths of planting, but this information is given for each subject in the descriptive lists of plants. Most are planted with a hand trowel or a special bulb planter – make sure that the base of the bulb, corm, etc, is in close contact with the soil. If there is a vacuum beneath, then rooting may not occur.

If drainage is poor it is not a bad idea to place a layer of coarse sand in each hole, especially for those subjects which like really well-drained conditions, such as lilies.

General care
With most of the subjects in this book the foliage dies down at some stage and the plants rest. It is absolutely vital that the foliage is not cut off until it has browned and died down naturally, for it is needed by the plant to build up the storage organs. If you intend growing bulbs in grass you must be prepared to leave the grass uncut until the leaves of the bulbs have withered.

As a general rule, it is a good idea to liquid feed bulbs and similar plants after flowering, particularly daffodils, tulips, crocuses, etc, as this helps the plants to build up their storage organs. Generally speaking, the larger the bulbs, corms, etc, by the time the leaves die down, the better will be the flowering the following year. Liquid feed fortnightly, using a general-purpose fertilizer. Also keep plants well watered until the foliage dies down.

Unless you want to save seeds it is good practice to remove the dead flower heads from all of these subjects, as there is no point in letting plants expend energy on seed production. Removing the dead flowers from dahlias ensures continuous flower production.

You will find that many of the plants described in this book are tender in some areas; they will not survive frosts. Some such as agapanthus, summer hyacinth and Kaffir lily can be left in the ground, though, if protected over the winter. They should be mulched with bracken, straw or dry leaves. Simply place a deep layer over the soil where the plants are situated, and to prevent the material from being blown away by the wind, place a sheet of wire netting, or nylon netting, over it and secure the edges with wooden pegs.

In areas prone to frosts, more tender subjects need lifting in autumn and storing over the winter in a frost-free place. Examples include peacock orchids, dahlias, gladioli, lapeirousia, Persian buttercups, Indian shot and begonias. Lift before the frosts commence, although dahlias can be left in the ground until frost blackens the foliage. Dry them off for a few days and then remove all adhering soil before storing in trays in a dry, frost-proof place. Replant in the spring as soon as the worst of the frosts are over.

Some storage organs are started into growth in early spring in a heated greenhouse before being planted out – dahlias, Indian shot and tuberous begonias are a few examples. Dahlia tubers are put into boxes of compost or peat and kept moist. Strong shoots will be produced and these can be used as cuttings to produce new plants. When a batch of new plants has been secured, the old plants can be discarded. Alternatively, dormant dahlias can be planted direct in the open ground in late spring. The new shoots should then emerge through the soil by the time the frost have finished. Indian shot is started into growth in a similar way and once new shoots have been produced are potted into suitable size pots of potting compost and grown on in the greenhouse, to be planted out when all danger of frost is over. This technique also applies to tuberous begonias. Indian shot is best stored in slightly moist peat over winter and begonia tubers in dry peat.

Propagation

Very few amateur gardeners propagate bulbs, corms, etc, but overcrowded clumps of permanent subjects should be lifted and split up when the plants are dormant. They can then be replanted at the correct spacings to give them more room to grow. Bearded irises should be lifted and divided after flowering, when the clumps become large. Replant divisions from the outside edges of each clump. Each division should consist of a piece of rhizome with a fan of leaves.

Pests and diseases

There are many specific pests and diseases, but these are the most common.

Slugs and snails Easily controlled by putting down slug pellets as soon as new shoots emerge through the soil.

Fungal rots Many subjects are prone to rotting, both in the ground and in store. If this problem occurs frequently, dip bulbs in a fungicide, such as benomyl, before planting. Storage organs rotting in store should be removed to prevent infection spreading to healthy ones. Dust those remaining with flowers of sulphur.

Eelworms They cause distorted, stunted growth of various bulbs including narcissus. Infected plants should be destroyed. Do not replant in the same piece of ground.

Soil-borne pests Leatherjackets, cutworms and the larvae of narcissus flies will attack bulbs. To control, drench the soil with an insecticide like gamma-HCH. Symptoms are generally poor growth and maybe wilting of foliage.

Viruses Many subjects can become infected, including lilies. Symptoms are stunted or distorted growth and leaf mottling or streaking. There is no cure and infected plants should be destroyed.

Rodents Mice often eat underground storage organs. Use one of the proprietary rodent baits.

Aphids Greenfly and other aphids infest the shoot tips of many subjects, sucking the sap and weakening the plant. Spray with a systemic insecticide as soon as seen.

Abbreviations

Cult: cultivation
ILLUS: illustration
P, D & D: pests, diseases and
disorders

Spp & Vars: recommended
species, their varieties,
cultivars and hybrids

Hardiness

The plants described in this
book, assuming normal
garden environmental
conditions and no provisions
for special winter protection,
have been graded approxi-
mately for hardiness, as
follows:

Ultra-hardy: generally able to
survive temperatures below
−29°C (−20°F), in some
cases to −40°C (−40°F) or
lower

Very-hardy: generally hardy
below −18°C (0°F), in some
cases to nearly −29°C
(−20°F)

Moderately to very hardy:
hardy to about −15 to
−18°C (5 to 0°F)

Moderately hardy: hardy to
below −6°C (21°F) and in
many cases to −12 to −15°C
(10 to 5°F)

Semi-hardy: able to withstand
frosts to −6°C (21°F) at
most (and in some cases
rather less)

Tender: not hardy below
−1°C (30°F), thus needing to
be moved under frost-free
cover over winter in most
places.

Peacock orchids

Graceful tender corms from
East Africa, related to, and
similar to gladioli. Plants are
1½–3ft(45–90cm) tall with
starry white fragrant flowers,
to 3in(8cm) across, in arching
spikes of up to ten flowers,
during late summer or early
autumn (good for cutting).
Leaves are upright and sword-
like. **Spp & Vars:** *A. bicolor*
(*Gladiolus callianthus*) is most
often represented in gardens
by the more sturdy variety
murielae ILLUS (*A. murielae*)
which has reddish-purple
markings in the centres of the
flowers. **Cult:** well-drained
soil in full sun; plant corms
3in(8cm) deep in spring; best
lifted overwinter in all but
mild areas. **P, D & D:** slugs,
storage rots.

Agapanthus

Generally moderately hardy, tuberous plants also known as African blue lilies or, mistakenly, lilies of the Nile. Most are 2–4ft(0.6–1.2m) tall with rounded heads, 6–12in (15–30cm) across, of funnel-shaped flowers in shades of blue or white, during late summer and early autumn. Leaves are strap-shaped, to 2ft(60cm) long, forming a dense clump. **Spp & Vars:** *A. campanulatus* has soft blue flowers (deeper in 'Isis') in rather flat heads. *A. orientalis* is semi-hardy with evergreen foliage and white to deep blue flowers; varieties (often listed under *A. africanus* or *A. campanulatus*) are moderately hardy, including 'Albus' (white), *flore pleno* (double), 'Mooreanus' (dwarf) and 'Snowball' (white). *A.* 'Headbourne Hybrids' ILLUS is a compact, moderately to very hardy seed strain (shades of blue). **Cult:** rich, well-drained, deep soil in warm sun; plant tubers 4in(10cm) deep (more in cold areas); mulch or lift overwinter. **P, D & D:** generally none.

Ornamental onions

Mostly very hardy easily grown bulbs related to the well-known culinary onions, but with decorative value in gardens. Flowers are small and often rather starry and appear generally in rounded, sometimes perfectly globular, clusters on upright leafless stalks (good for cutting; some may be dried). Leaves are narrow to strap-shaped and smell of onions if bruised.

Taller types are useful for beds and borders, especially between shrubs, or for containers; smaller types are ideal for edging and for rock gardens. They may self-seed. **Spp & Vars:** *A. aflatunense* is 2½–4ft(0.75–1.2m) tall with 3–4in(8–10cm) globular heads of pinkish-purple starry flowers in late spring. *A. albopilosum* ILLUS p 15 (*A. christophii*; Persian onion) is

Ornamental onions (continued)

$1\frac{1}{2}$–3ft(45–90cm) tall with
large 6–10in(15–25cm) open
flower heads in early summer;
the seed heads are good for
drying. *A. beesianum* is 1–$1\frac{1}{2}$ft
(30–45cm) tall with 2in(5cm)
wide nodding heads of blue or
purple bell-shaped flowers in
midsummer, above grass-like
leaves. *A. caeruleum* (*A.
azureum*) is $1\frac{1}{2}$–2ft(45–60cm)
tall, having 2–3in(5–8cm)
rounded heads of deep sky-
blue flowers in early- to midsummer. *A. flavum* is ultra-
hardy and likes hot sun;
plants are 8–12in(20–30cm)
or more in height, having
$1\frac{1}{2}$–2in(4–5cm) loose clusters
of yellow urn-shaped flowers
in midsummer above grassy
leaves. *A. giganteum* is
perhaps the most impressive
species, growing to 3–5ft
(1–1.5m) with huge 4–6in
(10–15cm) or more dense and
perfectly spherical heads of
rosy-lilac flowers in early- to
mid-summer. *A. karataviense*
is 8–16in(20–40cm) tall with
4in(10cm) globular heads of
dull pink to greyish-white

starry flowers in late spring
above attractive broad, blue-
green leaves. *A. moly* ILLUS
p 16 (golden garlic) is ulta-
hardy where summers are hot,
reaching 1–$1\frac{1}{2}$ft(30–45cm) in
height with small 2–3in
(5–8cm) clusters of flowers in
late spring or early summer.
A. neapolitanum 'Grandi-
florum' (daffodil garlic) is
moderately hardy, to $1\frac{1}{2}$ft
(45cm) tall with small, loose
clusters of white flowers in
late spring. *A. ostrowskianum*
(*A. oreophilum ostrowskianum*)
is ultra-hardy where summers

Ornamental onions (continued)

are hot, to 1ft(30cm) in
height and with 2in(5cm)
rounded heads of pink to
carmine starry flowers in
early summer; variety
'Zwanenburg' has the richest
colour. *A. pulchellum* ILLUS
p 17 is 1–2ft(30–60cm) tall
with graceful loose heads of
small reddish-violet flowers in
midsummer; variety 'Album'
is white. *A. roseum* needs a
warm sunny position, then
growing to 1½ft(45cm) with
pink starry flowers in loose
3–4in(8–10cm) globular
clusters in early summer. *A.
sphaerocephalum* is 2ft(60cm)
tall with grassy leaves and
egg-shaped 1in(2.5cm)
clusters of wine-purple
flowers in midsummer. *A.
tuberosum* (Chinese chives) is
20in(50cm) tall with flattish
clusters of dark-eyed white
flowers in late summer. *A.
zebdanense* is moderately
hardy, 12–20in(30–50cm) tall

and with 2in(5cm) clusters of
bell-shaped white flowers in
late spring. **Cult:** any well-
drained, even poor, soil in full
sun or partial shade; plant
bulbs 4–6in(10–15cm) deep in
autumn. Tall species may
need some support. Divide
large clumps after flowering.
P, D & D: slugs, fungal rots.

Belladonna lilies

Semi- to moderately hardy bulbs native to South Africa, reaching 2ft(60cm) in height when in flower. Beautifully fragrant, trumpet flowers, each up to 5in(12cm) across at the mouth, appear in clusters of 6–12 from late summer before the strap-shaped leaves develop. Leaves appear in late winter or early spring and die down completely in midsummer. The bulb is poisonous. **Spp & Vars:** *A. belladonna* ILLUS has pink flowers, often shaded heavier at the petal tips; varieties are 'Hathor' (white, ivory-cream to yellow in the throat) and 'Parkeri' (cor- rectly × *Amarygia parkeri*; vigorous and free-flowering with deep pink, yellow centred flowers). **Cult:** fertile, well-drained soil in a warm, sunny sheltered position (ideally against a south-facing wall); plant bulbs shallowly in frost-free areas or 6–8in(15–20cm) deep elsewhere; divide only in midsummer once leaves die. **P, D & D:** generally none.

Anemones

Mostly very hardy spring-flowering small plants with tuberous or rhizomatous roots. Flowers are generally bowl-shaped, sometimes starry, often backed by a collar of frilly leaves, and usually one per stem. Leaves are deeply incut and rather ferny. Plants are excellent for rock gardens, border edging and for lightly-shaded semi-woodland sites. Many of the taller types are excellent for cutting. **Spp & Vars:** *A. apennina* is 8in(20cm) tall and good for naturalizing, having clear deep blue 1½in(4cm) flowers in spring; varieties are 'Alba' (white; petals bluish on underside) and 'Plena' (double flowers). *A. blanda* ILLUS p 19 is 6in(15cm) tall, often naturalizing to form a large carpet, with profuse blue daisy-like 1½in(4cm) flowers in early spring above rather fleshy foliage; best grown in a warm, sheltered spot; varieties are 'Atro-caerulea' (dark blue), 'Blue Star' (larger flowers), 'Char-

mer' (rose-red), 'Pink Star' (pink; yellow centre), 'Radar' (rose-pink to red; white centre) and 'White Splendour' (pure white). *A. coronaria* De Caen (florists' anemone) varieties are moderately hardy, 6–12in(15–30cm) tall with rather poppy-like flowers to 3in(8cm) across in shades of blue, mauve, red and white, each with a black

Anemones (continued)

central boss, in spring (or almost all year if planted in succession); these include 'Hollandia' ('His Excellency'; scarlet), 'Mr. Fokker' (purple-blue), 'Sylphide' (rose-magenta) and 'The Bride'. *A. coronaria* St. Brigid varieties ILLUS p 20 are similar but double flowered, such as 'Lord Lieutenant' (deep blue), 'Mount Everest' (white), 'The Admiral' (magenta to violet) and 'The Governor' (scarlet). *A. × fulgens* 'St. Bravo' strain is similar to the De Caen varieties, with mixed colours and starry flowers. *A. narcissi-flora* is 1½ft(45cm) tall with clusters of 1in(2.5cm) white flowers, often flushed pink, in spring. *A. nemerosa* (European wood anemone) is ultra-hardy, to 8in(20cm) tall with glossy white 1in(2.5cm) star-like flowers in spring (good in light shade). **Cult:** moist, well-drained soil in sun or partial shade; like lime; plant

2in(5cm) deep in late summer or early autumn (protect florists' anemones overwinter with mulch or cloches). **P, D & D:** slugs, viruses.

Arisaemas

Mostly moderately to very hardy tuberous plants of the arum family grown for their curious flowers and lush leaves. True flowers are insignificant, but held on a fleshy spike (the spadix) and surrounded by a flower-like, hooded spathe. Red or orange berries often follow in autumn. **Spp & Vars:** *A. candidissimum* ILLUS BELOW LEFT is 1ft(30cm) tall, with 3in(8cm) spathes in early summer before the leaves appear. *A. sikokianum* ILLUS BELOW RIGHT is 1½ft(45cm) tall with 6in(15cm) spathes in late spring. *A. triphyllum* (*A. atrorubens*, N. American Jack-in-the-pulpit) is 1–2ft (30–60cm) tall with 4–7in (10–18in) purple-brown, white-veined spathes in early summer. **Cult:** moist, but well-drained, humus-rich soil in shade; plant tubers 4–6in (10–15cm) deep in autumn. **P, D & D:** generally none.

Arums

Moderately to very hardy
tuberous plants mostly with
lush spear-shaped leaves
developing in autumn or
early winter and curious
flowers in spring consisting of
a fleshy spike of insignificant
true flowers (the spadix)
within a flower-like sheath
(the spathe). **Spp & Vars:**
A. creticum ILLUS is 1½ft
(45cm) tall with 7in(18cm)
spathes. *A. italicum* is similar
in height with prominently-
veined leaves up to 1ft(30cm)
long and pale yellow-green
1ft(30cm) spathes often
marked purple, followed by
upright dense clusters of
conspicuous red fruits ;
varieties are 'Marmoratum'
and 'Pictum', both with grey-
marbled foliage. *A. pictum*
(*A. corsicum*) is 1ft(30cm) tall
with 7in(18cm) purple-black
spathes. **Cult:** moist, but well-
drained humus-rich soil in
sun ; plant tubers 4in(10cm)
deep in autumn. **P, D & D:**
generally none.

Baboon flower

A single species of South African corm, moderately to very hardy if appropriately treated in winter. Plants are 10in(25cm) tall with upward-facing funnel-shaped flowers, each to 1in(2.5cm) long, in dense upright spikes in spring. Leaves are pleated and hairy, generally rather sparse in numbers. Flowers may be cut. This is a useful plant for a rock garden or for the front of a sunny border. **Spp & Vars:** *B. stricta* ILLUS is sold generally as mixed-colour strains, having fragrant flowers in shades of pale blue, violet, reddish-mauve, or white. **Cult:** well-drained soil in full sun; plant corms 6in (15cm) in autumn. Corms may also be planted in pots in late summer for flowers from early winter if taken under cool glass. **P, D & D:** generally none.

Tuberous begonias

Popular summer bedding and container plants with large fleshy, asymmetrical leaves and showy, generally double flowers (male and female flowers separate, but on same plant; females mostly insignificant). **Spp & Vars:** *B. evansiana* (*B. grandis*) is moderately hardy (more so if protected in winter), growing to 2–3ft (60–90cm) tall with rounded glossy leaves, coloured red beneath and on the veins; drooping branches of 1½in (4cm) flesh-pink flowers appear throughout summer. *B. × tuberhybrida* is a complex group of tender hybrids, of variable habit and with flowers in a wide range of colours (except blues and mauves), including bicolours, generally 2–4in(5–10cm) across, in summer and early autumn. Hybrids are grouped according to flower shape and habit (double flowers unless stated): Camellia-Flowered ILLUS FAR RIGHT p 25 (rosette flowers to 6in[15cm] across; ruffled petals in Ruffled

Camellia); Fimbriata Plena (Carnation-Flowered; fringed flowers to 5in[12cm] across); Marginata ILLUS TOP p 24 (*B. crispa marginata* varieties; single or double flowers with

Tuberous begonias (continued)

an outer band of contrasting colour); Marmorata ILLUS LEFT p 25 (*B.* × *marmorata* varieties; similar to Camellia-Flowered, but flowers are rose-pink, spotted or blotched white); Multiflora ILLUS BELOW p 24 (*B.* × *multiflora maxima* varieties; compact and bushy with profuse single or double 2–3in[5–8cm] flowers); Pendula (*B.* × *lloydii*; trailing or pendent habit; smallish single or double flowers in prolific clusters; good for hanging baskets etc.); Picotee (similar to Camellia-Flowered, but flowers edged with a different shade of the main colour); Rosebud (flowers to 5in [12cm] across, like part-open rosebuds). **Cult:** moist, but well-drained peaty soil in sheltered sun or partial shade; plant tubers 2–3in(5–8cm) deep in late spring. Start hybrids into growth indoors two months before planting out; lift and store before first hard frosts. **P, D & D:** flower abortion, generally due to erratic watering.

Blackberry lily

A single species of rhizomatous plant, generally moderately hardy but very hardy in a warm sunny spot if well mulched in winter. **Spp & Vars:** *B. chinensis* ILLUS (*Pardanthus chinensis*; sometimes known as the leopard flower) is 3ft(90cm) tall with clusters of 2in(5cm), red-spotted salmon-orange flowers in summer, followed by pods which split to expose clusters of shiny black seeds. Leaves are iris-like. **Cult:** well-drained soil in full sun; plant rhizomes 3in(8cm) deep in spring; mulch in winter in colder areas, or lift in autumn and store frost-free. **P, D & D:** generally none.

Brodiaeas

Generally moderately to very hardy corms rather like ornamental onions (see pp 15–17) with clusters of starry to tubular flowers, mostly about 1½in(4cm) long/wide, on slender stems in spring and summer. **Spp & Vars:** *B. idamaia* ILLUS ABOVE RIGHT (firecracker flower) is a tufted plant, to 2ft(60cm) tall, flowering in early summer. *B. ixioides* (*Triteleia ixioides*, pretty-face) is 1–2ft(30–60cm) tall with clusters of starry yellow flowers in early spring. *B. laxa* ILLUS BELOW RIGHT (*Triteleia laxa*, grass nut) is 2ft(60cm) tall, having violet-mauve funnel-shaped flowers from spring; variety 'Queen Fabiola' is deep violet; *B.* × *tubergenii* is similar with blue-violet flowers. **Cult:** fertile, well-drained soil in sun; plant corms 4–6in(10–15cm) deep in autumn (spring where winters very cold). **P, D & D:** generally none.

Spring meadow saffron

A single species of very hardy dwarf corm, of crocus- or colchicum-like appearance, good for grouping in a rock garden or at the front of a border. **Spp & Vars:** *B. vernum* ILLUS (*Colchicum bulbocodium, Colchicum vernum*) is 4–6in(10–15cm) tall, having small clusters of up to three rose-violet funnel-shaped flowers, with clawed petals, on very short stalks, appearing in very early spring before the leaves develop; leaves are narrow and strap-shaped, dying down in early autumn. **Cult:** any well-drained soil in full sun; plant corms 3in(8cm) deep in early autumn; lift and divide every three or four years for best flowering. **P, D & D:** generally none.

Mariposa lilies

Very hardy corms with cup-shaped flowers in summer, for rock gardens or raised beds. **Spp & Vars:** *C. luteus* (yellow Mariposa lily) is 12–20in (30–50cm) tall with yellow 2in(5cm) flowers. *C. venustus* ILLUS (white Mariposa lily) is 10–24in(25–60cm) tall with 3in(8cm) cream, yellow, orange, red, lilac, purple and white flowers, all marked red.

Cult: very well-drained poor soil in full sun; plant 2in (5cm) deep; if soil is not dry after flowering (during dormant period) lift and store until autumn; mulch in winter. **P, D & D:** generally none.

Camasses

Very hardy moisture-loving bulbs native to N. America, with starry white to violet-blue flowers in upright spikes in late spring or early summer. Plants are good for borders or in wild gardens and for naturalizing in grass. **Spp & Vars:** *C. cusickii* is 3ft(1m) tall with large spikes of up to 300 pale lavender to violet-blue 1½in(4cm) flowers; bulbs are very large. *C. leichtlinii* is 3–4ft(1–1.2m) tall with creamy-white to deep blue 1½in(4cm) flowers; varieties are 'Atrocaerulea' (deep violet-blue) and 'Semiplena' (double, creamy-white). *C. quamash* ILLUS (*C. esculenta*, quamash, common camass) is shorter, 1½–2½ft (45–75cm) in height, with dense spikes of violet-blue, pale blue or white flowers and bluish-green foliage. *C. scilloides* (*C. fraseri*, eastern camass, wild hyacinth of US) is shortest, to 2ft(60cm) with smaller spikes of pale blue 1in(2.5cm) flowers and grassy

leaves. **Cult:** moist, loamy (or heavy) soil in semi-shade; plant bulbs 3–4in(8–10cm) deep in early autumn; dead head if self-seeding unwanted. **P, D & D:** generally none.

Indian shot

Mostly tall, semi- to moderately hardy rhizomatous
plants used mainly as dot
plants, adding tropical
elegance to summer bedding
schemes. **Spp & Vars:** *C. ×
generalis* (*C. × hybrida*)
hybrids are generally to 5ft
(1.5m) tall with crowded
spikes of flaring tubular
flowers, each to 4in(10cm)
across, in shades of red, pink,
orange, yellow and white in
summer to autumn; leaves are
up to 2ft(60cm) long and
green or bronze-purple.
Dwarf varieties to 2–2½ft
(60–75cm) are best for general
bedding and containers.
Varieties (tall and green-
leaved unless stated) include:
'Eureka' (cream), 'Lucifer'
(crimson, edged yellow),
'Nirvana' (dwarf; yellow;
red buds; variegated leaves),
'Pfitzer' series (dwarf; mixed),
'Red King Humbert' ILLUS
(very tall), 'Richard Wallace'
(canary-yellow), 'The
President' (scarlet), 'Tyrol'
(pink; bronze leaves) and
'Yellow King Humbert'

(yellow, marked red). **Cult:**
moist, but well-drained,
humus-rich soil in full sun;
start into growth indoors two
months before planting out,
4–5in(8–12cm) deep; dead-
head; lift and store before
first frosts. **P, D & D:**
generally none.

Giant lilies

Very hardy majestic bulbs
rather similar to lilies (see
pp 73–80) but with large
heart-shaped dark green
leaves. Flowers are large and
trumpet-shaped, predomi-
nantly white or creamy in
colour and held on sturdy
upright spikes in mid- to late
summer. **Spp & Vars**
(formerly classed as *Lilium*
spp): *C. cordatum* is 6ft(1.8m)
tall with spikes of up to 24
drooping 6in(15cm) long
flowers, marked reddish-
brown and yellow. *C. giganteum* ILLUS is similar, but
6–8ft(1.8–2.5m) tall. **Cult:**
humus rich, moist but well-
drained soil in cool shade;
plant bulbs shallowly in
autumn. Bulb dies after
flowering leaving offsets
which subsequently flower
within 3–5 years, so for
annual continuity of flowers
plant bulbs of varying age
(size) together. **P, D & D:**
generally none.

Chionodoxas

Very hardy, early-spring-flowering, dwarf alpine bulbs with clustered, upward-facing starry flowers. **Spp & Vars:** *C. gigantea* (*C. luciliae* 'Gigantea') is 8in(20cm) tall with white-eyed, pale- or gentian-blue 1½in(4cm) flowers; variety 'Pink Giant' is orchid-pink. *C. luciliae* ILLUS BELOW LEFT is very dwarf, to 3–6in(8–15cm), with tiny 1in(2.5cm) flowers; varieties are 'Alba' (white), 'Rosea' ILLUS BELOW RIGHT and 'Tmolii' (*C. tmolii*; almost stemless; pale blue; later). **Cult:** drained soil in sun; plant 3in(8cm) deep in autumn. **P, D & D:** slugs.

Kaffir lilies

Tender spring- or early summer-flowering evergreen plants with fleshy bulb-like roots, usually grown in pots or tubs under glass, but sometimes treated as garden plants in certain areas. Flowers are trumpet-shaped in large heads, on stout upright stems. Leaves are strap-shaped, to 2ft(60cm) long and rich, glossy green. **Spp & Vars:** *C. miniata* ILLUS is 1½ft(45cm) tall with 3in (8cm) long flowers. *C. nobilis* is shorter, to 1ft(30cm), with drooping, tubular-shaped, red and yellow, green tipped flowers. **Cult:** fertile, well-drained soil in semi-shade; plant shallowly in autumn. Only suitable for growing in areas which are frost-free during winter, or in slightly colder areas where some winter protection or mulch can be provided. **P, D & D:** generally none.

Colchicums

Very hardy, generally autumn-flowering showy corms resembling crocuses, and often known as autumn crocuses, though actually unrelated. Flowers are cup-shaped, white to purplish in colour, and appearing directly from the ground without any leaves. The leaves appear in spring and die down completely in early summer; they are much larger than the flowers, generally strap-shaped and glossy. Since the tufted foliage may be rather untidy, plants are best situated in a shrubbery or in rough grass; they will naturalize freely. Corms and seeds are poisonous. **Spp & Vars** (heights quoted refer to flowers only): *C. agrippinum* is 3–4in(8–10cm) tall with starry rose-purple and white chequered flowers. *C. autumnale* (autumn crocus, meadow saffron) is 6in(15cm) tall with 4in(10cm) wide lilac flowers; varieties are 'Album' (white), 'Major' (robust; lilac-mauve) and 'Minor' (small; rose-

lilac); *C. byzantinum* ILLUS p 35 (*C. autumnale major*) is similar. *C. speciosum* is 6in (15cm) or more in height with goblet-shaped, 4in(10cm) wide, rose-pink to purplish flowers from late summer; variety 'Atrorubens' ILLUS BELOW LEFT p 36 has reddish-purple flowers; hybrids with more robust flowers include

Colchicums (continued)

'Autumn Queen' (violet-purple), 'Disraeli' (dark mauve, faintly chequered), 'Lilac Wonder' (deep lilac-pink, striped white), 'The Giant' (larger violet-mauve flowers), 'Violet Queen' ILLUS BELOW RIGHT p 36 and 'Waterlily' (double, waterlily-like, lilac-mauve flowers).

C. luteum (yellow spring colchicum) is 4in(10cm) tall with yellow $1\frac{1}{2}$in(4cm) wide flowers in early spring. **Cult:** well-drained soil in sun or light shade; plant corms 3in (8cm) deep in mid- to late summer (when dormant). **P, D & D:** generally none.

Crinums

Generally semi- to moderately hardy bulbs with large clustered heads of trumpet-shaped, 3–4in(8–10cm) long, very fragrant flowers in summer and early autumn. The leaves are evergreen, rather untidy and up to 3ft (90cm) long. **Spp & Vars:** *C. moorei* is 4ft(1.2m) tall with rose-pink flowers and rather broad leaves; variety 'Album' ILLUS ('Schmidtii') has pure white flowers. *C. × powellii* is a moderately hardy hybrid between *C. moorei* and *C. bulbispermum* (a pink-flushed white species sometimes grown in gardens) having more profuse, reddish-pink to white flowers. A moderately hardy intergeneric hybrid with the related belladonna lily (see p 18), × *Crinodonna corsii* (× *Amarcrinum howardii*), is similar in habit to the crinums but with broader, clear pink trumpet flowers. **Cult:** rich, fertile, well-drained soil in warm sun; plant bulbs shallowly in frost-free areas or 6–8in(15–20cm) deep elsewhere. **P, D & D:** generally none.

Montbretias

Moderately to very hardy easily grown corms native to S. Africa with arching spikes of funnel-shaped, 1–2in (2.5–5cm) long flowers from midsummer (good for cutting) among sword-shaped semi-evergreen foliage. **Spp & Vars:** *C. aurea* (*Tritonia aurea*) is moderately hardy, 3ft(90cm) tall and yellow-flowered. *C. × crocosmiiflora* hybrids are 2–2½ft(60–75cm) tall with yellow to scarlet flowers in late summer; popular varieties are 'Citronella' (lemon-yellow), 'Emily McKenzie' (deep orange, crimson throat), 'Firebird' (flame), 'His Majesty' (scarlet, orange centre), 'Jackanapes' (yellow and orange bicolour), 'Lucifer' (taller; flame-red; early), 'Solfatare' (apricot; bronzed leaves), 'Spitfire' (orange) and 'Vulcan' ILLUS (deepest orange-red). *C. masonorum* is 2½ft(75cm) tall with broader, upward-facing orange-red flowers. *C. pottsii* is 4ft(1.2m) tall with yellow, red-flushed

flowers in more upright sprays. **Cult:** well-drained soil in full sun; plant corms 3in(8cm) deep in spring; trim back in spring. **P, D & D:** generally none.

Crocuses

Among the most popular and colourful dwarf corms, generally very hardy and flowering in late winter and early spring, though some in autumn and early winter. When in flower plants are usually 3–4in(8–10cm) tall (leaves may grow taller later). Flowers are upright and goblet-shaped, often opening starry or cup-shaped, in shades of blue, pink, lilac, purple, yellow or white. Leaves are grassy with a silvery centre vein, often expanding fully only after the flowers have faded. These are excellent plants for rock gardens, border edges, around the base of specimen trees, underplanting low ground cover plants and for containers; spring-flowering species are good for naturalizing in short grass (do not mow before leaves turn yellow).

Spp & Vars: LATE WINTER & SPRING FLOWERS – *C. ancyrensis* 'Golden Bunch' has profuse and long-lasting golden-tangerine flowers from

Crocuses (continued)

late winter. *C. chrysanthus* typically has profuse golden-yellow flowers in late winter though numerous varieties have other colours, including 'Advance' (pale yellow, marked bronze and mauve), 'Blue Pearl' ILLUS ABOVE p 39, 'Cream Beauty' ILLUS BELOW p 39, 'E. A. Bowles' (bright yellow, marked purple-bronze), 'Ladykiller' (white, marked purple-blue) and 'Zwanenburg Bronze' (golden-yellow and bronze). *C. etruscus* 'Zwanenburg' ILLUS ABOVE p 40 flowers from late winter. *C. sieberi* varieties, including 'Hubert Edelsten' ILLUS ABOVE p 41 and 'Violet Queen' (violet-blue), have beautiful starry flowers in late winter which appear before the leaves. *C. tomasinianus* is good for naturalizing, having flowers in mid- to late winter with slender lavender flowers which open almost flat; varieties include 'Ruby Giant' ILLUS BELOW p 40. *C. vernus* varieties (Dutch crocuses) have large flowers in early

Crocuses (continued)

spring up to 5in(12cm) tall;
they include 'Early Perfection'
(violet-blue), 'Joan of Arc'
(white), 'Large Yellow' ILLUS
BELOW p 41, 'Peter Pan'
(white), 'Pickwick' (silvery-
grey, striped deep lilac),
'Queen of the Blues'
(lavender-blue) and 'Van-
guard' (silvery-lilac).
AUTUMN & EARLY WINTER
FLOWERS – *C. kotschyanus* (*C.
zonatus*) has unusual rose-
lilac flowers in mid-autumn.
C. nudiflorus is a spreading,
early autumn flowering species
having purple blooms before
the leaves appear. *C.
speciosus* is up to 5in(12cm)
tall with lilac-blue, dark-
veined or speckled flowers in
mid-autumn. **Cult:** well-
drained soil in sun or light
shade; plant corms 3–4in
(8–10cm) deep in autumn
(spring types) or in early
summer (autumn types).
P, D & D: rodents and
leatherjackets eat corms;
birds damage flowers
(especially yellows).

Cyclamen

Dwarf very hardy, tuberous-rooted, shade-loving plants, generally 4–6in(10–15cm) tall, forming carpets of rounded heart-shaped leaves which are often marbled or blotched silver, and 2–3in(5–8cm) long. Characteristic nodding flowers with backswept petals, mostly ¾–1in(2–2.5cm) long, stand above the foliage on leafless stalks; colours range from white, through pink to crimson and violet. Plants are excellent for underplanting shrubs and trees, or for shady rock gardens. **Spp & Vars:** *C. coum* has all-green or silver-marbled foliage (latter often listed as variety *atkinsii*) and broad-petalled, purple-blotched pink, crimson or white flowers in winter and early spring. *C. europaeum* (*C. purpurascens*) has deep carmine flowers in summer above silver-marked leaves (red-purple beneath). *C. hederifolium* (*C. neapolitanum*) flowers in autumn before the leaves appear, having profuse rose-pink blooms (white in

variety 'Album' ILLUS); leaves are large and often rather lobed. **Cult:** moist, but well-drained peaty soil in full or partial shade; plant tubers 2in(5cm) deep (*C. hederifolium* very shallowly) in late summer or early autumn. Best to plant pot grown tubers as dry ones do not always establish. **P, D & D:** generally none.

Border dahlias

Tender tuberous plants with
showy flowers, 2–12in
(5–30cm) or more across, of
varied form and colour, from
midsummer to the first frosts
(good for cutting) in all
colours except blues, including many blends and bi-
colours. Leaves are rich mid-
green, sometimes bronzed.
Smaller varieties good for
bedding; taller types for
mixed borders etc. **Spp &
Vars:** *D. × cultorum* hybrids.
Single types are 1½–2½ft
(45–75cm) tall with small,
daisy-like flowers; mostly
raised from seed. Anemone-
flowered types ILLUS ABOVE
p 43 are 2–3½ft(0.6–1.1m) tall
with small flowers having a
pincushion-like central disc
of tubular petals. Collarette
types are 2½–4ft(0.75–1.2m)
tall with small flowers having
a collar of shorter, con-
trastingly coloured petals.
Decorative types ILLUS p 44
are 3–5ft(1–1.5m) tall with
miniature to giant, double
flowers; petals may be
regular (Formal) or irregular

Border dahlias (continued)

(Informal). Ball types are 3–4ft(1–1.2m) tall with small globular double flowers; Pompon types ILLUS BELOW p 43 are similar but with miniature flowers. Cactus types are 3–5ft(1–1.5m) tall with miniature to giant flowers having narrow, 'quilled' petals (broader in Semi-cactus). **Cult:** rich, well-drained but moist soil in sun; plant 4–6in(10–15cm) deep after last hard frost. Stake tall types; pinch out leading shoot at 3–4 weeks; dead-head. Lift tubers and store dry overwinter. **P, D & D:** aphids, borers, cutworms, earwigs (damage flowers), virus/fungal diseases.

Wand flowers, angel's fishing rods

Moderately hardy semi-evergreen corms with wiry arching stems carrying dangling trumpet-shaped flowers, each to 1in(2.5cm) long from midsummer into autumn. Leaves are very narrow and grass-like. **Spp & Vars:** *D. pulcherrimum* is 5–6ft(1.5–1.8m) tall with deep purplish-red flowers. *D. pendulum* ILLUS is similar, but smaller with white to mauve-pink flowers. **Cult:** well-drained soil in full sun; plant corms 3in(8cm) deep in spring; where not hardy lift corms in autumn and store frost-free. **P, D & D:** generally none.

Bluebells

Very hardy late-spring-flowering bulbs with upright spikes of mainly blue bell-shaped flowers (cuttable). Good for planting in groups in borders, wild gardens, on banks and under light trees and shrubs. **Spp & Vars:** *E. hispanicus* ILLUS (*Scilla campanulata, S. hispanicus,* Spanish bluebell) is 1–1½ft (30–45cm) tall with strong spikes of ¾in(2cm) violet-blue bells; varieties are 'Excelsior' (very large flowers; taller spikes), 'La Grandesse' (white), 'Myosotis' (clear blue; early), 'Queen of the Pinks' (deep pink) and 'White Triumphator' (white). *E. nonscriptus* (*Scilla nutans,* English bluebell) is shorter, to 1ft(30cm) with curving spikes of ½in(1cm) violet-blue flowers; varieties are 'Alba' (white) and 'Rosea' (pink). **Cult:** acid, humus rich, moist but well-drained soil in sun or shade (will tolerate alkaline soil); plant 3–4in(8–10cm) deep in autumn. **P, D & D:** generally none.

Pineapple lilies

Semi-hardy stately bulbs, mostly 2ft(60cm) tall with cylindrical heads of starry flowers on sturdy stalks topped with a leafy tuft, appearing in mid- to late summer from a rosette of arching leaves. **Spp & Vars:** *E. bicolor* has 1in(2.5cm) purple-edged green flowers and wavy leaves. *E..comosa* ILLUS has $\frac{1}{2}$in(1cm) lilac-centred greenish-cream flowers. **Cult:** well-drained sandy soil in sheltered sun or partial shade; plant 4–5in (10–12cm) deep in autumn (spring where not hardy and lift overwinter); good in pots. **P, D & D:** generally none.

Freesias

Tender to semi-hardy corms widely grown under cool glass for cut flowers, but suitable for growing outdoors in frost-free areas. Plants are up to 1½ft(45cm) tall with one-sided arching sprays of beautifully fragrant, waxy, funnel flowers, 1–2in(2.5–5cm) long, in a wide colour range from white and yellow to pink, red, orange and purple. Leaves are sparse and sword-shaped. **Spp & Vars:** *F. × hybrida* varieties include 'Aurora' (creamy-gold), 'Cote d'Azur' ILLUS BELOW RIGHT, 'Prince of Orange' (orange), 'Red Star' ILLUS BELOW LEFT, 'Romany' (double-flowered; mauve) and 'Venus' (rose, centred ivory). **Cult:** well-drained soil in sun; plant corms 3in(8cm) deep. In frost-free zones plant in late summer for flowers in late winter and spring; elsewhere plant prepared corms in spring for flowers from late summer (discard after flowering). Provide twiggy support. **P, D & D:** aphids.

Fritillaries

Mostly very hardy spring-flowering bulbs with drooping bell-shaped flowers, generally 1in(2.5cm) across, appearing singly or in clusters near the top of stems. Leaves are mostly narrow or lance-shaped, dying down in mid-summer. **Spp & Vars:** *F. imperialis* (crown imperial fritillary) is a good 'dot' plant, growing 2–3ft(60–90cm) tall with yellow or red, musty-scented flowers on a strong upright stem and below a leafy 'crown'; varieties are 'Aurora' (orange-red), 'Lutea Maxima' (lemon-yellow) and 'Rubra Maxima' (burnt orange). *F. meleagris* (snake's head fritillary; guinea-hen flower) is ultra-hardy, to 12–16in(30–40cm) tall with chequered white and reddish-purple flowers; varieties include 'Aphrodite' (white) and 'Artemis' ILLUS. *F. persica* is 3ft(90cm) tall with spikes of ¾in(2cm) violet-blue flowers; variety 'Adiyaman' is purple and taller. **Cult:** humus-rich,

moist but well-drained soil in partial shade; plant bulbs 4–6in(10–15cm) deep (*F. imperialis* deeper) in early autumn. Divide and replant every few years. **P, D & D:** generally none.

Snowdrops

Very to ultra-hardy bulbs
flowering mainly in winter or
early spring, also sometimes
known as fair maids of
February. Plants are mostly
6–8in(15–20cm) tall and with
nodding white bell-shaped
flowers to $\frac{3}{4}$–$1\frac{1}{4}$in(2–3cm) long
(cuttable). Alternate petals
are shorter than the others
and frequently marked green.
Leaves are rather blue-green
and strap-shaped. Popular for
naturalizing in short grass and
for planting under trees and
large shrubs. **Spp & Vars:**
G. caucasicus is ultra-hardy
with rounded flowers from
mid-winter. *G. elwesii* (giant
snowdrop) is 10in(25cm) tall
with larger flowers from late
winter. *G. nivalis* (common
snowdrop) is ultra-hardy,
flowering from mid-winter;
varieties are 'Atkinsii' ILLUS
(larger flowers; very early),
'Flore Pleno' (double), 'Sam
Arnott' (taller; fragrant) and
'Straffan' (flowers in mid-
spring); *G. n. reginae-olgae*
flowers in autumn before the

leaves appear and prefers an
open position. **Cult:** moist,
rich soil in partial shade; best
planted 4in(10cm) deep in
spring when growing (bulbs
resent drying out). **P, D & D:**
generally none.

Summer hyacinth

Moderately to very hardy bulb to 4ft(1.2m) tall with sturdy upright spikes of nodding 1½in(4cm) bell-shaped flowers in late summer. Leaves are narrow and strap-shaped. Plants, also known sometimes as spire lilies, are good for the back of borders and for cutting. **Spp & Vars:** *G. candicans* ILLUS (*Hyacinthus candicans*) with green-tinged white flowers is the only species cultivated. **Cult:** any well-drained fertile soil, preferably in full sun; plant bulbs 6in(15cm) deep in spring. Lift bulbs overwinter in cold areas ideally, though a thick mulch in winter may provide adequate protection. **P, D & D:** generally none.

Gladioli, sword lilies

Very popular and showy summer-flowering corms with tall one-sided spikes of irregular, outward-facing trumpet-shaped flowers in a wide range of colours and bicolours. Leaves are dark green, sword-shaped and ribbed, and held very upright. Plants are good for grouping in mixed borders and for cutting. **Spp & Vars:** *G. byzantinus* is very hardy, to 2ft(60cm) tall with open spikes of reddish-purple, rose-pink or white 2½in(6cm) flowers in early summer. *G.* × *colvillei* varieties, sometimes sold incorrectly as *G. nanus*, are moderately hardy, to 1½–2ft(45–60cm) tall with loose spikes to 10in(25cm) long of upward-facing 3in (8cm) flowers in early summer, scarlet blotched yellow in original hybrids; other varieties are 'Amanda Mahy' (salmon), 'Peach Blossom' ILLUS p 52, 'Spitfire' (scarlet blotched lilac) and 'The Bride' (white). *G.* × *hortulanus* (garden gladiolus) varieties

are grouped by flower form (sold as mixtures and hundreds of named varieties): Large-Flowered Hybrids ILLUS p 53 are semi-hardy, growing to 3–4ft(1–1.2m) tall

Gladioli, sword lilies (continued)

with vigorous habit and strong 16–20in(40–50cm) dense spikes of rather triangular 4–7in(10–18cm) flowers in mid- to very late summer; the colour range is very wide, often with a contrasting throat, edging or blotching; Primulinus Hybrids are 2–3ft(60–90cm) tall with slender spikes to 16in(40cm) long of hooded 2–3in(5–8cm) flowers in midsummer, mostly in softer shades; Butterfly Hybrids are 2–3ft(60–90cm) tall with dense spikes to 1½ft(45cm) long of 2–4in(5–10cm) flowers often with ruffled petals and striking throat markings. **Cult:** well-drained fertile soil in sun; plant corms 4–6in(10–15cm) deep in mid- to late spring (in succession every two weeks for best display). Lift semi-hardy types before the first hard frost and overwinter frost-free. **P, D & D:** insects and fungal diseases in store.

Blood lilies

Tender to semi-hardy bulbs with dense clusters of tiny flowers, each with prominent stamens, in summer. Leaves are oblong or lance-shaped. Plants are best grown in containers except in very warm climates. **Spp & Vars:** *H. coccineus* is up to 10in (25cm) tall when in flower with 3in(8cm) brush-like red flower heads appearing before the leaves develop. *H. katharinae* (blood flower) is 1ft(30cm) tall with 6in(15cm) round heads of salmon-red flowers. *H. multiflorus* ILLUS is 1½ft(45cm) tall with 6in (15cm) flower heads. **Cult:** rich, well-drained soil in sun; plant shallowly in spring; keep under cover in winter. **P, D & D:** generally none.

Hyacinths

Mostly very hardy spring-flowering bulbs with upright cylindrical spikes of bell-shaped flowers and fleshy strap-shaped leaves. **Spp & Vars:** *H. orientalis* hybrids (Dutch hyacinths) are 10–12in (25–30cm) tall with dense spikes to 6in(15cm) long of heavily fragrant flowers with reflexing waxy petals in mid- to late spring; varieties are numerous in shades of blue, pink, yellow and white, including 'Ostara' ILLUS. *H. orientalis albulus* (Roman/French-Roman hyacinth) is moderately to very hardy, 6–8in(15–20cm) tall with loose heads of white, pink or blue reflexing flowers in early spring; *H. romanus* (*Bellevalia romana*, Roman/Dutch-Roman hyacinth) is similar with blue-tinged white flowers in mid- to late spring. **Cult:** well-drained soil in sun; plant bulbs 2–3in(5–8cm) deep (Dutch hyacinths 6in [15cm] deep) in autumn. **P, D & D:** generally none.

Bearded irises

Striking though short season, very hardy rhizomatous-rooted plants for border display; dwarfs for rock gardens. Flowers are ruffled with a 'beard' of fleshy hairs on the lower petals ('fall petals') and appear, several to a stem, in succession in spring or early summer. The colour range is very wide, flowers often being bicoloured. Leaves are sword-like and grey-green in colour, forming an upright fan; they are semi- or fully evergreen. Plants spread slowly by swollen stems (rhizomes) which may be cut into pieces when dormant and replanted to increase numbers. Bearded irises are classified into two groups: Cushion types flower in late spring and have a broad cushion-like beard; True Bearded types are sub-divided by height and flower size. **Spp & Vars:** MINIATURE DWARF BEARDED TYPES are up to 8in(20cm) tall with 2–3in (5–8cm) flowers in mid-spring – *I. chamaeiris* has yellow, white or purple flowers in pairs or singly. *I. pumila* is just 4in(10cm) tall with stemless purple, white or yellow

Bearded irises (continued)

flowers. Hybrids include 'Bee Wings' (yellow, brown patch), 'Blue Doll' (lavender-blue), 'Boo' (white and violet), 'Campbellii' (violet), 'Chieftain' (blue-black), 'Laced Lemonade' (yellow; wavy petals), 'Little Buccaneer' (red and orange), 'Moonlight' (pale yellow), 'Pixie' (cream and bronze) and 'Ritz' (yellow and maroon). STANDARD DWARF BEARDED TYPES are 8–16in(20–40cm) tall with 3–4in(8–10cm) flowers in mid-spring – Hybrids include 'Blue Denim' ILLUS RIGHT p 56, 'Bronze Babe' (yellow and bronze), 'Church Stoke' (purple), 'Gingerbread Man' (brown and purplish), 'Gleaming Gold' (brassy-yellow), 'Green Spot' ILLUS LEFT p 56, 'Melon Honey' (apricot and white), 'Red Heart' (lavender-blue and

Bearded irises (continued)

dark red), 'Regards' (pink and maroon) and 'Sweetie' (pink). INTERMEDIATE & BORDER BEARDED TYPES are 16–28in (40–70cm) tall with 4–5in (10–12cm) flowers in late spring or early summer – Hybrids include 'Apache Warrior' (golden-tan and red), 'Chiltern Gold' (yellow), 'Dummer Boy' (light blue and deep blue), 'Frenchi' (orchid-pink and rose-violet), 'Lang-port' series (various colours), 'Little Reb' (purple and white), 'Scintilla' (cream) and 'Red Orchid' (dark red and gold). TALL BEARDED TYPES are 28–48in (70–120cm) tall with 4–7in (10–18cm) flowers in early summer – *I. germanica* (flag iris, fleur-de-lys) is evergreen with purple and white flowers. Hybrids include 'Blue-Eyed Brunette' (brown and blue), 'Christmas Time' (white and red), 'Credo' (maroon and bronze), 'Dream

Bearded irises (continued)

Lover' (blue-white, purple
and lemon), 'Dusky Dancer'
(black-violet), 'Eleanor's
Pride' (pale blue), 'Gaylord'
(white and purple), 'Golden
Alps' (ivory and yellow),
'Gypsy Jewels' (rich red),
'Latin Lover' (white veined
purple and deep purple),
'Olympic Torch' (copper-
bronze), 'One Desire' ILLUS
p 57, 'Radiant Apogee'
(yellow, white and brown),
'Raspberry Ripples' (raspberry pink and red), 'Rippling
Waters' (pale violet-blue and
red), 'Rondo' (white and red-
violet), 'Royal Touch' ILLUS
p 58, 'Sea Captain' (sky-
blue), 'Spreckles' (yellow
speckled red), 'Touché' (pink
and blue), 'Tuxedo' ILLUS
p 59, 'West Coast' (orange-
gold) and 'Wild Apache'
(cinnamon, violet, white and
wine-red). CUSHION TYPES are
variable in height and flower
size – *I. hoogiana* is 20in
(50cm) tall with lavender-
blue 4in(10cm) flowers in
twos or threes. *I. stolonifera* is
2ft(60cm) tall with 3in(8cm)

Bearded irises (continued)

brown, blue marked flowers; variety 'Zwanenburg Beauty' is blue, edged bronze with maroon-flushed fall petals. *I. susiana* (mourning iris) is 16in(40cm) tall with solitary grey flowers, 4–5in(10–12cm) across, veined and blotched dark purple. The hybrid 'Thor' ILLUS p 60, an Oncogelia variety, is 1½ft(45cm) tall with 4–5in(10–12cm) flowers;

'Chione' is similar, but with bluish-white and brown flowers. **Cult:** grow bearded irises in free-draining, more or less neutral soil in full sun; plant firmly, leaving the top of the rhizome just exposed. Divide plants every 3–4 years, after flowering, and discard the woody centre. **P, D & D:** slugs, snails, bud flies, borers, rots, scorch.

Beardless irises

Rhizomatous plants similar to bearded irises (pp 56–60) in habit, but the elegant flowers lack a 'beard' on their lower petals ('fall petals'). The flowers are often bicoloured and delicately marked or veined, being held several to a stem (many good for cutting). Leaves are long and rather narrow; mostly evergreen. Plants are good for moist borders; smaller types for rock gardens. Beardless irises are classified into several groups: Pacific Coast irises are moderately to very hardy with dainty 2½–4in(6–10cm) flowers in late spring and early summer; Louisiana swamp irises are moderately hardy spreading plants with 3–4in(8–10cm) flowers usually grouped on zigzag stems in early- to mid-summer; Siberian (Sibirica) irises are mostly very hardy with profuse 2½–4in(6–10cm) flowers in groups on slender stems in early summer above grass-like herbaceous leaves; Spuria irises are mostly very hardy and clump-forming with robust, waxy 2½–6in (6–15cm) flowers in early summer among blue-green

Beardless irises (continued)

reed-like foliage. **Spp & Vars:**
PACIFIC COAST IRISES – *I.
douglasiana* ILLUS LEFT p 61
is 20in(50cm) tall with lilac-
purple, lavender, buff or
whitish flowers. *I. innominata*
is 8in(20cm) tall with golden-
yellow, buff or cream flowers.
I. tenax (Oregon iris) is 16in
(40cm) tall with lavender-
blue, cream or pink flowers.
Pacific Coast hybrids ILLUS
RIGHT p 61 are 10–16in
(25–40cm) tall with branched
stems of blue-purple, red,
yellow or white flowers; sold
mainly in mixtures or by
colour. LOUISIANA SWAMP
IRISES – *I. fulva* ILLUS p 62
(copper iris) is 2ft(60cm) tall
with copper or pinkish
flowers. Louisiana hybrids are
2–3ft(60–90cm) tall with
showy 5–8in(12–20cm)
flowers, including 'Dixie Deb'
(pale yellow), 'Pristine
Beauty' (turquoise-blue) and
'Wheelhorse' (red). SIBERIAN
IRISES – *I. chrysographes* is
2ft(60cm) tall with violet-blue
or reddish-purple flowers,
veined gold. *I. forrestii* ILLUS

LEFT p 63 is 16in(40cm) tall, or
more in wet soil, with pale
yellow flowers, veined brown
on the falls. *I. sibirica* varieties are ultra-hardy with
branching stems to 3ft(90cm)
tall; flowers are up to 6in
(15cm) across; varieties
include 'Cambridge' (light
blue), 'Cleve Dodge' (velvety

Beardless irises (continued)

black-purple), 'Ewen' ILLUS RIGHT p 63, and 'Sea Shadows' (blue and turquoise). SPURIA IRISES – *I. orientalis* (*I. ochroleuca*) is ultra-hardy, to 4ft(1.2m) tall with cream and gold flowers; *I. spuria* is shorter with bluish-purple flowers. Spuria hybrids (butterfly irises) are 3–4ft (1–1.2m) tall having a wide colour range, but generally only suitable for warm climates; they include 'Contradiction' ILLUS RIGHT p 64;

some moderately hardy varieties are available. OTHER BEARDLESS IRISES – *I. foetidissima* ILLUS LEFT p 64 (gladdon, stinking gladwyn) is moderately to very hardy, to 1½ft (45cm) tall with pale purple flowers followed by large pods which split to reveal scarlet seeds (dryable). *I. kaempferi* (*I. ensata*, Japanese iris) is very hardy, to 3ft(90cm) tall with broad-petalled 4–8in(10–20cm) flowers in clusters in mid-

Beardless irises (continued)

summer and deciduous leaves; varieties are 'Hercules' (dark blue), 'Kagari Bi' (rose-pink) and 'Variegata' (violet; variegated leaves). *I. unguicularis* (*I. stylosa*, Algerian iris) is moderately to very hardy with short-stemmed solitary lilac flowers all winter; leaves grow to 2ft (60cm) in summer. **Cult:** grow most beardless irises in moist, neutral or lime-free soil in full sun; plant rhizomes 1–2in (2.5–5cm) deep. Siberian irises like cool, rich soil and are tolerant of semi-shade; Spuria irises are tolerant of any soils; *I. foetidissima* tolerates dry shade; *I. unguicularis* prefers poor dryish alkaline soil (good at foot of wall). **P, D & D:** as for bearded irises (see p 60).

Crested irises

Rhizomatous plants similar to bearded and beardless irises (pp 56–64) in habit, but the flowers are flattish in shape with a showy fringed 'crest' on the lower petals ('fall petals'). Flowers are paler and less vivid than previous irises, often pastel-coloured. Leaves are generally sword-shaped and evergreen. Larger species are good for borders; small species for rock gardens. **Spp & Vars:** *I. cristata* (dwarf crested iris) is ultra-hardy and deciduous, reaching just 4–8in(10–20cm) in height, having pale lilac 2½in(6cm) flowers with white and orange crests in mid-spring. *I. japonica* 'Ledger's Variety' ILLUS is very hardy, to 2ft(60cm) tall with 2–3in (5–8cm) flowers on branched stems in late spring. **Cult:** humus-rich, lime-free soil in semi-shade; plant rhizomes of *I. japonica* just below the surface, those of *I. cristata* partly exposed. **P, D & D:** as for bearded irises (see p 60).

Bulbous irises

Herbaceous irises growing from a bulb rather than a rhizome as in other groups (pp 56–65). The flowers are rather elegant and mostly with slender petals. Many make good container plants. Bulbous irises are classified into three main groups: Juno irises are generally moderately to very hardy and of distinctive form, having upright leafy stems and four or more 3in(8cm) flowers per stem in spring (the lower 'fall' petals are much larger than the others); Netted irises (Reticulata irises) are very hardy with 3in(8cm) flowers in late winter (earliest of all irises), tubular leaves and fibrous-netted bulbs; English, Dutch & Spanish irises are moderately hardy with 4–5in (10–12cm) flowers in ones or twos (good for cutting) and rather sparse reed-like leaves.

Spp & Vars: JUNO IRISES – *I. aucheri* is 1ft(30cm) tall with lavender-blue, pale green streaked, fragrant flowers. *I. bucharica* ILLUS p 66 is 1½ft(45cm) tall with cream and gold flowers. NETTED IRISES – *I. danfordiae* ILLUS RIGHT p 67 is dwarf, to 5in (12cm) tall, having bright yellow flowers before the leaves appear. *I. histrioides* 'Major' is also 5in(12cm) tall with gentian-blue, white-spotted flowers before the leaves (ideal for pots).

Bulbous irises (continued)

I. reticulata varieties and hybrids are 6in(15cm) tall, including 'Cantab' ILLUS LEFT p 67, 'Harmony' (sky-blue; flowers before leaves), 'Joyce' (sky-blue), 'J. S. Dijt' (red-purple; fragrant) and 'Pauline' (red-violet). *I. winogradowii* is very dwarf, to just 4in(10cm) tall with lemon-yellow flowers before the leaves. ENGLISH, DUTCH & SPANISH IRISES – *I. xiphioides* (English iris)

hybrids are 2ft(60cm) tall, having white, blue, purple or pink flowers. *I. xiphium* (*I. hispanica*, Spanish iris) hybrids ILLUS LEFT p 68 are 1–1½ft(30–45cm) tall with yellow, bronze or purple flowers. Dutch hybrids (Dutch irises) are 16–24in(40–60cm) tall with white, blue or purple flowers in early summer; named hybrids include 'Bronze Queen' (golden brown and bronze, flushed blue), 'Lemon Queen' ILLUS RIGHT p 68, 'Professor Blaauw' (mid blue, marked yellow), 'Royal Yellow' (yellow, falls richer yellow), 'Sunshine' (yellow),

Bulbous irises (continued)

'Wedgwood' (pale blue) and 'White Excelsior' (white, streaked greenish-yellow). **Cult:** grow bulbous irises in light, well-drained soil in full sun in a sheltered spot; Juno and Netted irises need alkaline soil. Plant bulbs of Juno irises 2in(5cm) deep, Netted irises 3in(8cm) deep and English, Dutch & Spanish irises 4in(10cm) deep, all in early autumn (protect the latter in winter in cold areas). Dead-head and feed after flowering. **P, D & D:** grey bulb rot, ink disease and mosaic virus; mice eat bulbs.

African corn lilies

Moderately hardy corms
native to South Africa,
growing to 1½ft(45cm) in
height. Flowers are star-
shaped to 1½in(4cm) across in
upright spikes on wiry stems
from late spring to early
summer or later (good for
cutting; pick when just open).
Leaves are narrow and sword-
shaped, and rather sparse.
Plants are best grown in
containers which can be
moved under protection
overwinter in cold areas. **Spp
& Vars:** *Ixia* hybrids ILLUS are
often listed as *I. viridiflora*,
though are actually derived
from various species. A wide
colour range is available,
mostly with a contrasting
central eye, sold as unnamed
seedlings and varieties
including 'Afterglow' (buff-
orange; centre rimmed red-
black), 'Hogarth' (creamy-
yellow; purple centre),
'Nelson' (white; purple-red
centre), 'Rose Emperor' (soft
pink; carmine-pink centre),
'Uranus' (deep yellow;

maroon eye) and 'Vulcan'
(red and burnt orange). **Cult:**
any well-drained soil in full
sun; plant corms 3in(8cm)
deep in autumn, or in spring
for later flowers. Provide
some winter protection in
colder areas. **P, D & D:**
generally none.

Lapeirousias

Moderately hardy corms native to South Africa, related to and similar to freesias (see p 48). Plants are 1ft(30cm) tall with starry trumpet-shaped flowers to 1in(2.5cm) wide in one-sided, arching spikes from mid-summer (can be forced under glass for winter flowers). Leaves are narrow and pointed, forming a flattened fan. Best grown in containers which can be moved under protection overwinter in cold areas. **Spp & Vars:** *L. laxa* ILLUS (sometimes spelled *Lapeyrousia laxa*; *Anomatheca cruenta*) has pinkish-red flowers, shaded darker in the centre. *L. grandiflora* is similar, but larger. **Cult:** any well-drained fertile soil in full sun in a sheltered spot; plant corms 3in(8cm) deep in spring. Lift corms in autumn and store frost-free where not fully hardy. **P, D & D:** generally none.

Snowflakes

Very hardy bulbs with
nodding white and green
flowers like snowdrops (see
p 50) though they are more
rounded with petals all the
same length (good for cutting). **Spp & Vars:** *L. aestivum*
ILLUS (summer/giant snow-
flake, Loddon lily) is 1½–2ft
(45–60cm) tall with arching
clusters of ¾–1in(2–2.5cm)
flowers in late spring; variety
'Gravetye Giant' is robust
with larger flowers. *L.
autumnale* (autumn snow-
flake) is 10in(25cm) tall with
pink-flushed ½in(1cm)
flowers in late summer to
autumn, and grass-like leaves.
L. vernum (spring snowflake)
is 8in(20cm) tall with ¾in(2cm)
flowers in late winter or early
spring; leaves are strap-
shaped; *L. v. carpathicum* has
yellow-marked flowers. **Cult:**
moist soil in sun or partial
shade; plant 3–4in(8–10cm)
deep in autumn. (*L. autumnale*
should be planted just 2in
[5cm] deep in well-drained
soil in full sun in early spring).
P, D & D: generally none.

Libertias

Moderately hardy rhizomatous plants to 3ft(90cm) tall. Flowers are rounded, white and greenish in colour in branching spikes, opening from brownish buds in late spring to early summer. Leaves are rather grass-like. **Spp & Vars:** *L. formosa* ILLUS has ¾in(2cm) flowers. *L.* *ixioides* is similar but smaller. **Cult:** acid (lime-free) well-drained soil in full sun; plant rhizomes 3in(8cm) deep in early autumn. Where hardy leave in ground overwinter, protecting with mulch or a cloche if necessary, otherwise lift in autumn and store frost-free. **P, D & D:** generally none.

Lilies

Among the most important and stately of all bulbs, with elegant, often beautifully fragrant flowers, mostly in early summer. Leafy stems are crowned with six-petalled flowers which may be trumpet-shaped, flat or reflexing (latter known as 'Turk's-cap' flowers) with protruding prominent pollen-bearing stamens, and held singly or in loose clusters (very good for cutting). Leaves are mostly narrow and lance-shaped. Bulbs are generally large and scaly (scales may be detached and grown on in pots, eventually producing new plants) and many grow roots also from the stem above the bulb and so must be planted deeply. Plants are suitable for mixed borders and among shrubs or in woodland-type gardens; some can be grown in pots. Eight divisions of hybrids are classified (according to flower shape and parentage); a ninth division holds all the true species. Consult a specialist catalogue

for the innumerable named hybrids. **Spp & Vars** (all very hardy and early summer-flowering unless stated): SPECIES – *L. amabile* ILLUS p 73 is ultra-hardy, to 3ft(1m) tall with spikes of up to six pendant, red Turk's-cap flowers to 3in(8cm) across; variety 'Luteum' is orange-

Lilies (continued)

yellow. *L. auratum* ILLUS p 74 (gold-rayed/gold-banded lily) is moderately hardy, to 5–8ft(1.5–2.5m) tall with spikes of up to 35 crimson-spotted white flowers each up to 1ft(30cm) across and banded golden-yellow, in late summer; variety 'Rubrum' is banded crimson. *L. candidum* ILLUS p 75 (madonna lily) is 4–5ft(1.2–1.5m) tall with spikes of 5–20 waxy pure white trumpet-shaped, very fragrant flowers to 3in(8cm) long; leaves appear in autumn and persist over winter (likes some lime; plant shallowly). *L. hansonii* is 4ft (1.2m) tall with large spikes of nodding, orange-yellow flowers to 2½in(6cm) wide, spotted brown and with strongly reflexed petals (lime

Lilies (continued)

hater). *L. henryi* is up to 8ft (2.5m), requiring staking; arching stems hold loose clusters of 4–20 fragrant, orange-yellow to apricot, reflexed flowers to 3½in(9cm) long in mid- to late summer. *L. longiflorum* (white trumpet/ Easter lily) is moderately hardy, to 3ft(1m) tall with small clusters of horizontal, very fragrant, white trumpet flowers each 5–7in(12–18cm) long, in midsummer; variety 'Holland's Glory' is hardier. *L. martagon* (Turk's-cap lily) is ultra-hardy, to 3–5ft (1–1.5m) tall with spaced rings of foliage topped by a large spray of unpleasantly-scented Turk's-cap flowers, each to 1½in(4cm) long and usually purple-pink spotted black. *L. regale* (regal/royal

Lilies (continued)

lily) is ultra-hardy, to 4–6ft
(1.2–1.8m) tall with crowded
leaves and loose clusters of up
to 30 horizontal, fragrant
trumpet flowers in mid-
summer, each to 6in(15cm)
long and white shaded yellow
and rose-purple. *L. speciosum*
(Japanese lily) is moderately
to very hardy, to 4–5ft(1.2–
1.5m) tall with broad leathery
leaves and very large leafy
sprays of nodding bowl-
shaped flowers in very late
summer, each to 6in(15cm)
wide with reflexing petals
coloured waxy-white and
heavily shaded crimson or
rose with raised crimson
spots; varieties are 'Ellabee'
(pure white), 'Grand Com-
mander' ILLUS p 76 and
'Rubrum' (carmine-red,
edged white). *L. tigrinum*
(tiger lily) is ultra-hardy, to
4–6ft(1.2–1.8m) tall with
clusters of up to 25 nodding
Turk's-cap, brilliant orange-
red flowers, each to 5in(12cm)
across and with purple-black
spots (lime hater); varieties
are *L. t. flaviflorum* ILLUS p 77

(yellow tiger lily) and
'Splendens' (larger, rich-red
flowers with bold spots).
ASIATIC HYBRIDS – Generally
compact plants derived from
Asiatic species, to 2–4ft(0.6–
1.2m) tall; division is sub-

Lilies (continued)

divided by flower shape and carriage. Those with upward-facing flowers include the *L. × hollandicum* varieties (candlestick lilies) with cup-shaped red, orange or yellow 3½in(9cm) flowers. Mid-Century and other hybrids have reflexed flowers to 4–5in (10–12cm) across in a wide colour range with maroon or brown spots, held in broad clusters. Outward-facing hybrids, having reflexed spotted flowers, also include some of the Mid-Century Hybrids together with the Preston Hybrids (lime hating). Pendent hybrids are generally similar to those above, but have pendent Turk's-cap spotted flowers, each to 3–4in

Lilies (continued)

(8–10cm) across and held on long stalks; major groups are Fiesta Hybrids (large trusses of yellow to dark red flowers) and Harlequin Hybrids (taller plants with a wide range of flower colours).

MARTAGON HYBRIDS – 5–6ft (1.5–1.8m) plants with sprays of 20–30 pendent Turk's-cap flowers, each to $1\frac{1}{2}$in(4cm) long. *L. × backhousiae* varieties (Backhouse Hybrids) have white, yellow, pink or maroon flowers, marbled or spotted pink or purplish such as 'Marhan' ILLUS p 78.

BELLINGHAM HYBRIDS – Similar to Martagon hybrids, but with larger 3in(8cm) flowers in shades of yellow, orange and red (including bicolours), all prominently spotted brown, such as 'Afterglow' ILLUS p 79.

TRUMPET & AURELIAN HYBRIDS – Sub-divided by flower shape. Trumpet-shaped hybrids are generally 5–6ft(1.5–1.8m) tall with candelabra-like clusters, of 12–20 trumpet flowers, each

to 8in(20cm) long, in mid-summer; varieties and strains are numerous in a wide colour range, including the sturdy and lime-tolerant Olympic Hybrids. Pendent hybrids are 4–6ft(1.2–1.8m) tall with strong stems holding

Lilies (continued)

clusters of nodding trumpet- or bowl-shaped flowers in late summer. Star-shaped hybrids are 4–6ft(1.2–1.8m) tall with rather flat starry flowers, each to 7in(18cm) wide, in clusters in mid-summer. ORIENTAL HYBRIDS – Very beautiful plants derived from Japanese species, with huge spotted and generally bicoloured flowers in large clusters in mid- to late summer; they need richer and well-drained soil in full sun. Bowl-shaped hybrids are 3–5ft tall with bowl-shaped flowers to 10in(25cm) across, such as 'Crimson Beauty' ILLUS p 80. Star-shaped hybrids are 5–7ft(1.5–2m) tall with starry flattish flowers to 10in(25cm) across, having recurving tips. Recurved hybrids are 4–6ft(1.2–1.8m) tall with large loose clusters of

Lilies (continued)

strongly recurved flowers to 7in(18cm) wide. **Cult:** grow most in well-drained (but not dry) soil with ample humus in sun or partial shade; plant 4–6in(10–15cm) deep in autumn or early spring (if soil is heavy plant in a pocket of sand). Even very hardy types are best protected with thick mulch below about 0°F (−18°C). **P, D & D:** rodents and squirrels eat bulbs; slugs, various insects, viruses, fungal diseases.

Spider lilies

Semi- to moderately hardy bulbs with funnel-shaped, waxy-petalled flowers in rounded clusters during late summer. Leaves are strap-shaped, dying down in summer before the flowers appear. **Spp & Vars** (all sometimes listed as *Amaryllis* spp): *L. aurea* (golden spider lily) is 1½ft(45cm) tall with 3in(8cm) golden-yellow flowers. *L. radiata* ILLUS BELOW LEFT (red spider lily) is 16in(40cm) tall with 1½in(4cm) spidery flowers. *L. squamigera* ILLUS BELOW RIGHT (*Amaryllis halii*, resurrection lily, autumn amaryllis) is very hardy if the summers are hot, but otherwise moderately hardy, growing to 2ft(60cm) tall with 3in(8cm) flowers in large clusters. **Cult:** rich, fertile, well-drained soil in a warm, sunny site; plant bulbs shallowly in midsummer. Protect in winter with mulch. **P, D & D:** generally none.

Butterfly irises

Semi- to moderately hardy iris-like corms, sometimes also known as Natal lilies, giving a succession of showy but short-lived, fragrant iris-like flowers on branching stems from late spring to summer. Leaves are narrow and rather sparse. **Spp & Vars:** *M. irioides* (*Dietes vegeta*, African iris) is 3ft(90cm) tall with white and yellow flowers, marked blue. *M. ramosissima* (*M. ramosa*) is moderately hardy, growing to 2ft(60cm) tall with yellow flowers shaded blue. *M. tricuspidata* ILLUS (peacock iris) is 2ft (60cm) tall with pure white flowers, marked peacock-blue. **Cult:** well-drained soil in full sun; plant corms 3in (8cm) deep in autumn in a warm spot. Protect with mulch over winter where not fully hardy. **P, D & D:** generally none.

Grape hyacinths

Very to ultra-hardy dwarf
bulbs related to the Dutch
hyacinths (p 55) but with
much smaller spikes of tiny
$\frac{1}{4}$–$\frac{1}{3}$in(5–8mm) urn-shaped or
globular flowers (cuttable),
generally in mid-spring,
among grassy foliage.
Excellent for naturalizing
(multiply freely) and for
edging and rock gardens.
Spp & Vars: *M. armeniacum*
is 10in(25cm) tall with
tapering spikes of white-
edged cobalt-blue flowers;
leaves appear in autumn and
overwinter; varieties are
'Blue Spike' ILLUS LEFT p 83
(large double flowers),
'Cantab' (pale blue), 'Early
Giant' (large flowers) and
'Heavenly Blue' (sky-blue).

Grape hyacinths (continued)

M. botryoides (common grape hyacinth of Europe) is 8in (20cm) tall with white-rimmed deep blue flowers; variety 'Album' ILLUS RIGHT p 83 is white. *M. comosum* (tassel hyacinth) is 1–1½ft (30–45cm) tall with loose spikes of olive-green flowers topped by a tuft of upright purple flowers, in late spring; varieties 'Monstrosum' and 'Plumosum' (feather hyacinths) have violet-blue and reddish-purple flowers respectively, with shredded petals giving a feathery effect. *M. macrocarpum* ILLUS LEFT p 84 (*M. moschatum flavum*) is 8in (20cm) tall with long arching leaves and bright yellow flowers. *M. racemosum* ILLUS RIGHT p 84 (*M. moschatum*, musk hyacinth) is 8–10in (20–25cm) tall, flowering in early- to mid-spring; *M. tubergenianum* (Oxford & Cambridge grape hyacinth) is similar with tapering spikes of dark blue flowers topped with pale blue flowers. **Cult:** well-drained soil preferably in sun; plant bulbs 2–3in (5–8cm) deep in early autumn.
P, D & D: generally none.

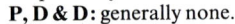

Wild daffodils and narcissi

Species, natural varieties and wild hybrids from which the familiar garden daffodils and narcissi are derived. Mainly dwarf, mostly very hardy, small-flowered spring-flowering bulbs, generally with one flower per stem (good for cutting) in shades of yellow, cream and white; flowers consist of an inner trumpet- or cup-shaped 'corona' surrounded by a collar of petals (the perianth). Plants are ideal for rock garden pockets, pots and containers, or for naturalizing in short grass (most increase prolifically in good soil). **Spp & Vars:** *N. asturiensis*

Wild daffodils and narcissi (continued)

(*N. minimus*) is the smallest
trumpet daffodil, to just
3–5in(8–15cm) tall with 1in
(2.5cm) long golden-yellow
flowers in late winter. *N.
bulbocodium* (hoop-petticoat
daffodil) is 6in(15cm) tall
when in flower, having 1in
(2.5cm) conical trumpets and
very narrow petals from late
winter; *N. b. citrinus* has
lemon-yellow flowers in very
early spring; *N. b. conspicuus*
is similar, but with larger
deep yellow flowers. *N.
cyclamineus* ILLUS LEFT p 88
(cyclamen-flowered narcissus)
is 6–8in(15–20cm) tall with
golden, drooping and narrow
trumpets with backswept
petals in very early spring
(best in moist light shade).
N. jonquilla ILLUS p 85
(jonquil) is 1ft(30cm) tall with
clusters of $1\frac{1}{4}$–$1\frac{1}{2}$in(3–4cm)
wide, small-cupped, fragrant
flowers in mid-spring. *N.
lobularis* is 4–6in(10–15cm)
tall with small pale yellow
flowers in late winter;
N. obvallaris ILLUS p 86
(*N. pseudonarcissus obvallaris.*

Wild daffodils and narcissi (continued)

Tenby daffodil) is similar, but
taller, to 1ft(30cm) with bright
golden 1½–2in(4–5cm)
trumpets in late winter to
early spring. *N. × odorus* (*N.
campernellii*, campernelle
jonquil) is 12–16in(30–40cm)
tall with small clusters of
bright yellow, 2½in(6cm)
wide, bell-shaped fragrant
flowers in mid-spring;
N. campernellii plenus (Queen
Anne's Irish campernelle) has
double flowers. *N. poeticus*
ILLUS p 87 (poet's/pheasant's-
eye narcissus) is 16–18in
(40–45cm) tall with 2–3in
(5–8cm) wide white flowers in
late spring, having a red-
rimmed, short cup; *N. p.
recurvus* ('Old Pheasant's
Eye') has backswept petals.
N. pseudonarcissus (wild
daffodil, Lent lily) is a
variable species, 6–12in
(15–30cm) tall with 2–2½in
(5–6cm) yellow trumpets
surrounded by paler petals, in
early spring. *N. tazetta*
(bunch flowered/polyanthus
narcissus) is semi- to moderately hardy, to 1–1½ft

Wild daffodils and narcissi (continued)

(30–45cm) tall with clusters of 1–2in(2.5–5cm) white flowers in winter, each with a very shallow pale yellow cup; variety 'Paper White' (*N. t. papyraceus*) is pure white and the earliest narcissus, often grown in pots indoors.

N. triandrus (angel's-tears narcissus) is 8in(20cm) tall with clusters of pendulous white to yellow flowers in early spring, each with a ¾in (2cm) globular cup and back-swept petals; the typical variety is *albus* ILLUS RIGHT

p 88 with creamy-white flowers, growing to just 3–4in (8–10cm) tall. **Cult:** any, preferably rich, well-drained soil in sun or dappled shade; plant bulbs 3–4in(8–10cm) deep in late summer to early autumn. Dead-head. Lift and divide clumps when very large. **P, D & D:** eelworms, narcissus fly grubs, basal rot.

Garden daffodils and narcissi

Hybrids of the wild daffodils and narcissi (see pp 85–88), mostly of complex parentage and generally taller with showier flowers in shades of yellow, orange, cream and white, appearing singly (unless stated below) in spring. Leaves are strap-shaped and greyish-green. These are among the most favoured spring bedding plants; also for naturalizing in grass or for borders and containers. Hybrids are classified by flower form and by origin into 12 divisions, and sometimes sub-divided by colour and cup size. Some 15,000–20,000 varieties are recognised, a selection of which are listed below. **Spp & Vars:** TRUMPET DAFFODILS – Generally 14–18in(35–45cm) tall; their

Garden daffodils and narcissi (continued)

flowers have large trumpets which are at least as long as the petals; early/mid season. All-yellow varieties include 'Arctic Gold', 'Dutch Master' ILLUS p 89 (very large flowers), 'Golden Harvest' and 'Unsurpassable' (very large flowers). Bicoloured varieties with cream or white petals and yellow trumpets include 'Goblet', 'Magnet' and 'Queen of Bicolours' (canary-yellow). All-white varieties are 'Beersheba', 'Mount Hood' (trumpet opens creamy-yellow) and 'W. P. Milner' (dwarf; yellowish). Reversed bicoloured varieties with the trumpet paler than the petals include 'Spellbinder' (greenish-yellow; trumpet becoming white). LARGE-CUPPED NARCISSI – Generally to 16–20in(40–50cm) tall; their flowers have a cup-shaped, often ruffled trumpet of $\frac{1}{3}$ but less than $\frac{1}{2}$ the petal length; early/mid season. All yellow varieties are 'Carlton' (soft yellow), 'Galway', 'Hyperion' (sulphur-yellow, cup shaded

pale orange) and 'Yellow Sun'. Yellow varieties with an orange or reddish cup include 'Confuoco' (cup scarlet), 'Fortune' (cup coppery orange-red) and 'Scarlet

Garden daffodils and narcissi (continued)

O'Hara' (cup scarlet). White
varieties with a yellow cup are
'Brunswick', 'Duke of
Windsor' (cup orange-
yellow), 'Green Island' ILLUS
p 90 (cup greenish-yellow)
and 'Rococo' (cup apricot to
yellow, centred ivory). White
varieties with orange to red
cups are 'Flower Record' (cup
dark orange at rim), 'Professor Einstein' (orange flat
cup) and 'Sempre Avanti'
(creamy with orange cup).
White varieties with a pinkish
cup or trumpet (colour best in
sun) include 'Mrs R. O.
Backhouse' (narrow apricot
and shell-pink trumpet) and
'Salmon Trout' (salmon-pink
trumpet). All white varieties
are 'Easter Moon' (green eye)
and 'Ice Follies' (cup opens
lemon-yellow). Reversed
bicoloured varieties with
petals darker than the cup
include 'Binkie' (sulphur-
yellow shading to white).
SMALL-CUPPED NARCISSI –
Generally 14–18in(35–45cm)
tall; their flowers have a
small cup, less than $\frac{1}{3}$ the

length of the petals; mid
season. Yellow-petalled
varieties are 'Birma' (cup
orange-scarlet) and 'Edward
Buxton' (cup orange, rimmed
darker). White-petalled
varieties include 'Barrett
Browning' ILLUS p 91, 'La
Riante' (cup deep orange-

Garden daffodils and narcissi (continued)

red) and 'Verger' (cup orange-red). All-white varieties are 'Polar Ice' and 'Verona'.

DOUBLE NARCISSI – Generally 14–18in(35–45cm) tall with double flowers, often sweetly scented; mostly mid-season. Varieties are *albus plenus odoratus* (double white Poeticus narcissus; late spring), 'Cheerfulness' ILLUS p 92 (multi-flowered; creamy-white; moderately hardy), 'Flower Drift' (semi-double; creamy-white, orange centre), 'Golden Ducat' (large golden flowers), 'Texas' (tall; large yellow and orange flowers) and 'Van Sion' ILLUS LEFT p 93 (very early spring).

TRIANDRUS NARCISSI – Derived from *N. triandrus* (see p 88); generally 10–12in (25–30cm) tall with drooping flowers having silky back-swept and twisted petals; usually multi-flowered; mid/late season. Long-cupped varieties with the cup at least $\frac{2}{3}$ the petal length are 'Liberty Bells' (soft yellow), 'Thalia' (tall; pure white) and

'Tresamble' (white tinged cream). Short-cupped varieties include the dwarf 'April Tears' (deep yellow) and 'Hawera' (lemon-yellow).

CYCLAMINEUS NARCISSI – Cyclamen-flowered narcissi derived from *N. cyclamineus* (see p 86); generally 8–10in (20–25cm) tall with drooping,

Garden daffodils and narcissi (continued)

backswept, narrow flowers; early spring. Varieties are 'February Gold' ILLUS RIGHT p 93, 'Jack Snipe' (cream with gold trumpet), 'Peeping Tom' (taller; golden-yellow with darker trumpet) and 'Tete-a-Tete' (multi-flowered; golden). JONQUILS – Derived from *N. jonquilla* (see p 86); to 1–1½ft(30–45cm) tall with scented, broad-petalled and shallow flowers; usually multi-flowered; mid season. Varieties include 'Golden Sceptre' (golden-yellow), 'Suzy' (bright yellow; orange cup), 'Sweetness' (cream; yellow cup) and 'Trevithian' ILLUS LEFT p 94. TAZETTA & POETAZ NARCISSI – Polyanthus narcissi derived from *N. tazetta* and *N. poeticus* (see pp 87–88); vigorous and upright plants to 1½ft(45cm) tall with small scented flowers having a very short cup and often with crinkled petals; multi-flowered; early/mid season. Variety 'Geranium' ILLUS RIGHT p 94 is popular; 'Silver Chimes' is white with a creamy-lemon cup. POETICUS NARCISSI – Poet's narcissi

Garden daffodils and narcissi (continued)

derived from *N. poeticus* (see p 87 and very similar. Varieties are 'Actaea' (yellow cup), 'Cantabile' (green cup) and 'Old Pheasant's Eye' (see p 87). SPLIT-CORONA NARCISSI – Generally to 14–18in (35–45cm) tall; their flowers have a split cup separated into distinct petals and usually flat against the outer petals.

Varieties include 'Baccarat' (lemon-yellow) and 'Parisienne' (white with orange split cup). **Cult, P, D & D:** as for wild daffodils and narcissi (see p 88). Do not cut the leaves until dead; tie up only if essential. Apply a foliar-feed to plants grown on poorer soils or those in containers.

Nerines

Elegant bulbs mostly to 2ft(60cm) tall, having trumpet-shaped red, pink or white flowers with narrow, often wavy or frilly petals and prominent stamens, appearing in late summer to autumn. Leaves develop after the flowers have faded. **Spp & Vars:** *N. bowdenii* ILLUS is moderately hardy with large heads of 3in(8cm) flowers; varieties are 'Fenwick's Variety' (vigorous; large deep pink flowers), 'Pink Beauty' (deep pink) and 'Pink Triumph' (silvery-pink). *N. flexuosa* is semi-hardy with 2in(5cm) pale pink flowers. *N. sarniensis* (Guernsey lily) is semi-hardy with 3in(8cm) vermilion to crimson flowers. **Cult:** rich, fertile, well-drained soil in full sun; plant bulbs 4–6in(10–15cm) deep in early summer. **P, D & D:** generally none.

Nomocharis

Graceful lily-like Himalayan
bulbs growing well only in
cool, moist climates, but
otherwise very hardy.
Flowers are bell- or saucer-
shaped, often nodding, and
held at the top of leafy stems
in midsummer. **Spp & Vars:**
N. aperta ILLUS is 2–3ft
(60–90cm) tall with slightly
nodding 4in(10cm) flowers.
N. farreri is 3ft(90cm) or
more in height with nodding
3in(8cm) white flowers
centred with a maroon eye
and spotted purple. *N.
pardanthina* is 2–3ft(60–90cm)
tall with sprays of up to ten
nodding, saucer-shaped pale
pink flowers, each to 3in(8cm)
wide, the inner petals rounded
and fringed with heavy
purple spotting. *N. saluenen-
sis* is 3ft(90cm) tall with
rather starry saucer-shaped
pale rose flowers, each to
3½in(9cm) wide with a dark
red-purple eye and freckles
and the petals flushed deeper
pink at their tips. **Cult:** moist,
peaty soil in semi-shade;

plant bulbs 6in(15cm) deep in
spring (stems root above the
bulb so essential to plant
quite deeply). Mulch well in
winter. Plants resent dis-
turbance once established.
P, D & D: slugs, snails.

Stars of Bethlehem

Generally sun-loving bulbs with clusters or spikes of starry white flowers and narrow, often grassy leaves. Many are often grown in pots under glass but all are suitable for growing outdoors in appropriate climates where they may naturalize; taller types in a mixed border, dwarf types in a rock garden or for edging. **Spp & Vars:** *O. arabicum* ILLUS BELOW p 97 (*O. corymbosum*) is moderately hardy, 1½–2ft (45–60cm) tall with flattish clusters of 2½in(6cm) flowers, each with a black centre, in late spring (bulbs need hot summers to ripen for following year's flowers). *O. balansae* ILLUS BELOW p 00 is very hardy, to 4–6in(10–15cm) tall with small starry flowers in early- to mid-spring. *O. nutans* ILLUS ABOVE p 97 is very hardy, to 1–1½ft (30–45cm) tall with one-sided spikes of nodding starry flowers, striped green on their reverse, each to 2in(5cm) across, in spring (cuttable).

Stars of Bethlehem (continued)

O. thyrsoides (chincherinchee) is semi-hardy, to 2ft(60cm) tall with clusters of 1in(2.5cm) flowers in early spring where hardy (elsewhere plant in spring for flowers in summer); an excellent plant for long-lasting cut flowers. *O. umbellatum* is very hardy, 8–12in(20–30cm) tall with flattish heads of 1in(2.5cm) flowers striped green on their reverse, in late spring; naturalizes freely and may become weedy. **Cult:** any well-drained soil in sun (*O. nutans* in semi-shade); plant bulbs 2–3in(5–8cm) deep in autumn where hardy, elsewhere in spring (lift in autumn and store frost-free over winter). **P, D & D:** generally none.

Wood sorrels

Mostly moderately hardy, low-growing dainty plants with bulbous roots forming mats or tufts of clover-like leaves and funnel-shaped 5-petalled flowers, often opening wide only in sun. Leaves may close up at night with the flowers. Plants are good for rock gardens; shade lovers for woodland-type situations. **Spp & Vars:** *O. adenophylla* is 4in(10cm) tall with 1¼in(3cm) lilac-pink, maroon-centred flowers from late spring, above grey-green foliage. *O. braziliensis* is 4in(10cm) tall forming a carpet of purplish foliage with purplish-red 1in(2.5cm) flowers in late spring. *O. deppei* (good-luck plant) is 6–10in(15–25cm) tall with cross-shaped, reddish-brown-blotched leaves and profuse carmine-pink to purplish-red flowers in small clusters in early summer; varieties are 'Alba' (white flowers) and 'Iron Cross' ILLUS p 99 (carmine flowers and bold leaf markings). *O. enneaphylla* is very hardy, to 3in(8cm) tall and tuberous-rooted; early summer flowers

Wood sorrels (continued)

are 2in(5cm) across, white in the species, but pale pink in variety 'Rosea' ILLUS p 100; the foliage is grey-green and fan-like. *O. laciniata* is very hardy and very dwarf, to just 2–4in(5–10cm) in height, rhizomatous, grey-green leaves and pale lavender-purple, dark-veined 1in (2.5cm) flowers in early summer. *O. lasiandra* is 6in (15cm) tall with clusters of crimson flowers in early summer above red-stalked leaves. *O. lobata* is tuberous, to 4in(10cm) in height with bright green leaves which die down in summer and are followed in autumn by golden-yellow flowers. *O. rubra* (*O. rosea*, *O. floribunda*) is tuberous, to 8in(20cm) tall with large clusters of deep pink $\frac{1}{2}$in(1.5cm) flowers from late spring (good for containers). **Cult:** well-drained but moist peaty and gritty soil in a warm sunny spot; plant 3in(8cm) deep – early-flowers in autumn, others in spring. **P, D & D:** generally none.

Tuberose

A single species of tender
tuberous plant best grown in
a container under glass and
moved outdoors during the
summer months. Plants are up
to 3½ft(1.1m) tall with spikes
of waxy pure white, funnel-
shaped flowers, each to 2½in
(6cm) long, in late summer to
autumn. Leaves are grassy, to
1½ft(45cm) long. The tuberose
is favoured chiefly for the
beautiful fragrance of its
flowers and can be forced
under glass for flowering at
almost any time in the year.
Spp & Vars: *P. tuberosa* has
single flowers; its variety 'The
Pearl' ILLUS has double
flowers and is more commonly
cultivated. **Cult:** light soil in a
warm sunny site; plant tubers
2in(5cm) deep in spring.
P, D & D: generally none.

Striped squill

A single species of very- to ultra-hardy small bulb related to, and similar to, the true squills (see pp 106–107). Plants are 4–8in(10–20cm) tall with slender spikes of 6–12 very pale blue open bell-shaped flowers in spring, each about $\frac{1}{2}$in(1cm) across and striped with a narrow band of blue on each petal. Leaves are strap-shaped. Striped squills are good for planting in groups in borders and in wild gardens, and especially on banks or in rock garden pockets. **Spp & Vars:** *P. libanotica* ILLUS (*P. scilloides libanotica*) is usually grown; its variety 'Alba' has pure white flowers. **Cult:** humus-rich, moist but well-drained gritty soil in sun or partial shade; plant bulbs 3–4in (8–10cm) deep in autumn. **P, D & D:** slugs.

Persian buttercups

Moderately hardy tubers of the buttercup family growing to 10–16in(25–40cm) in height with profuse semi-double or double 2–5in (5–12cm) flowers over a long season. Flowers are often several to a stem and in shades of yellow, orange, pink, red and white (good for cutting). Leaves are fresh-green and ferny; they die down in winter. According to the climate plants may be grown for flowers from late winter or in late spring and summer. **Spp & Vars:** *R. asiaticus* ILLUS is usually sold as mixed-colour tubers. **Cult:** humus-rich, very well-drained soil in full sun; plant tubers with their 'claws' downwards, 2in(5cm) deep in autumn where winters are mild for flowers in late winter, or in early spring elsewhere and lift in late summer (store cool and dry over winter).
P, D & D: generally none.

Romuleas

Moderately hardy crocus-like dwarf corms with clusters of starry flowers which open out, in early spring, only in sunshine. Leaves are slender and grass-like. Plants are good for group planting, naturalizing freely, and for rock garden pockets; they may also be grown in pots and containers. **Spp & Vars:** *R. bulbocodium* ILLUS is 6in(15cm) tall usually with bright purple, yellow-throated flowers opening to 1¼in(3cm) wide. *R. requienii* is shorter, to just 4in(10cm) in height with deep violet ¾in(2cm) wide flowers. **Cult:** well-drained fertile soil in full sun; plant corms 3in (8cm) deep in autumn.

P, D & D: generally none.

Kaffir lilies

Moderately hardy rhizomatous plants native to South Africa, growing to 2½ft(75cm) in height with upright spikes of starry cup-shaped flowers, each to 1½in(4cm) across, in late autumn (good for cuttings; sometimes known as crimson flags). Leaves are long and sword-shaped. **Spp & Vars:** *S. coccinea* has crimson flowers; varieties are 'Major' (larger flowers), 'Mrs Hegarty' (rose-pink), 'November Cheer' (pink), 'Salmon Charm' (flesh-pink) and 'Viscountess Byng' ILLUS. **Cult:** moist soil in a sunny sheltered position; plant 4in (10cm) deep in spring. Mulch in winter in cold areas; divide plants every four years. **P, D & D:** generally none.

Squills, scillas

Dwarf bulbs with bell-shaped to starry flowers, mainly in shades of blue, in spikes or rounded clusters on slender stems from late winter. Plants spread freely and are good for naturalizing on banks or for rock garden pockets. **Spp & Vars:** *S. bifolia* ILLUS p 106 (twinleaf squill) is very- to ultra-hardy, growing to 6–8in (15–20cm) in height with clusters of $\frac{1}{2}$in(1cm) gentian-blue flowers from late winter or early spring; leaves are narrow and typically two per bulb, sometimes three; varieties are 'Alba' (white) and 'Rosea' (shell-pink). *S. peruviana* (Cuban lily) is semi- to moderately hardy, to 1ft(30cm) tall with dense rounded heads of up to 100 deep blue $\frac{1}{2}$in(1cm) flowers in late spring and early summer. *S. pratensis* (meadow squill) is 10in(25cm) tall with dense spikes of tiny violet-blue bell flowers in spring to early summer. *S. sibirica* (Siberian squill) is ultra-hardy, to 8in (20cm) tall with loose spikes

of 2–5 brilliant violet-blue $\frac{1}{2}$in(1cm) nodding starry bell flowers in very early spring; varieties are 'Alba' (white), 'Atrocoerulea' ('Spring Beauty'; very early; larger, deeper blue flowers) and 'Taurica' ILLUS LEFT p 107 ('Multiflora'; very early;

Squills, scillas (continued)

paler flowers veined dark blue). *S. tubergeniana* ILLUS RIGHT p 107 is ultra-hardy, to 3–4in(8–10cm) tall with loose spikes of up to four very pale blue, open bell flowers to $1\frac{1}{2}$in(4cm) across and striped mid-blue, appearing from late winter just ahead of the leaves; variety 'Zwanenburg' has more pronounced striping. **Cult:** humus-rich, moist but well-drained soil in sun or shade; plant bulbs 3–4in (8–10cm) deep in autumn (*S. peruviana* in summer). **P, D & D:** eelworms, smut.

Jacobean/Aztec lily

A single species of semi-hardy bulb native to Mexico. Plants are 1–1½ft(30–45cm) tall with striking solitary red flowers to 4in(10cm) across in early summer. Leaves, to 1ft(30cm) long, develop after the flowers. **Spp & Vars:**

S. formosissima ILLUS, sometimes listed as *Amaryllis formosissima*. **Cult:** rich, fertile but well-drained soil in warm sun; plant 4–6in (10–15cm) deep in spring (autumn in warm areas). **P, D & D:** generally none.

Sternbergias

Moderately to very hardy
dwarf bulbs to 6in(15cm) tall
with rather crocus-like yellow
flowers, though held on short
stems, and strap-shaped
foliage. Plants are best suited
to rock gardens. **Spp & Vars:**
S. clusiana ILLUS (*S. macran-*
tha) has 3in(8cm) long goblet-
shaped golden-yellow flowers
in late summer to autumn;
leaves die down in summer
before the flowers appear.
S. fischerana has canary-
yellow 1½in(4cm) flowers in
spring along with the leaves.
S. lutea (*S. aurantiaca*,
Amaryllis lutea, autumn/
winter daffodil) may be the
biblical 'lily of the field',
having rich golden-yellow
1½–2in(4–5cm) flowers in
early autumn; leaves appear
along with or slightly after the
flowers. **Cult:** very well-
drained soil in full sun; plant
bulbs 4–6in(10–15cm) deep in
mid- to late summer.
P, D & D: generally none.

Tiger flowers

Moderately hardy bulbs from Central America with showy and distinctive spotted and striped flowers, sometimes called shell flowers. Plants are 1½–2ft(45–60cm) tall with 4–6in(10–15cm) wide flowers in mid- to late summer, each consisting of three broad outer petals opening flat, and a central cup of heavily marked, narrow pointed petals; they are rather short-lived but open in succession. Leaves are upright and pleated. **Spp & Vars:** *T.*

pavonia ILLUS is sold mainly as unnamed seedlings in shades of yellow, orange, lilac, red or white, all with brown or red central spotting; named varieties are 'Liliacea' (reddish-purple marked white), 'Lutea' (yellow), 'Rubra' (orange-scarlet) and 'Speciosa' (scarlet marked yellow) **Cult:** rich and fertile well-drained, though never dry soil in full sun; plant bulbs 3in(8cm) deep in spring (or in autumn where winters are mild). **P, D & D:** generally none.

Tritonias

Moderately hardy corms native to South America, growing to 1–1½ft(30–45cm) tall with broadly funnel-shaped flowers to 1½in(4cm) wide in arching spikes in late spring to early summer (good for cutting). Leaves are narrow and sword-shaped. Sometimes listed as *Crocosmia* or *Montbretia* spp and often called montbretias (see also p 38). **Spp & Vars:** *T. crocata* varieties include 'Incomparable' (deep orange); 'Isabella' (flesh-pink, tinged yellow), 'Roseline' (pink), 'Salmon Queen' ILLUS, 'Tea Rose' (cream, yellow centre) and 'White Glory' (white, tinged amber). **Cult:** well-drained soil in full sun; plant 3in(8cm) deep in autumn where hardy, otherwise best grown in pots and over-wintered under glass. Bulbs need warm summers to ripen satisfactorily. **P, D & D:** generally none.

Species tulips

Mostly very hardy showy bulbs from which the better-known garden tulips have been bred, but equally desirable spring plants. Flowers are goblet-shaped, sometimes opening flat (sizes below refer to flower length before fully open); most are held one to a stem (unless stated). Leaves are usually lance-shaped and rather grey- or blue-green. Ideal for rock gardens, small beds and borders, or for containers; many can be naturalized.

Spp & Vars: *T. acuminata* ILLUS p 112 (*T. cornuta*, horned/Turkish tulip) is 20in(50cm) tall with 3in(8cm) flowers in mid- to late spring. *T. aucherana* ILLUS p 113 is very dwarf, to 4in(10cm) tall with 1¼in(3cm) fragrant flowers in early spring. *T. biflora* is 4–6in(10–15cm) tall with ¾in(2cm) yellow-centred white flowers, shaded green and red on the outside and opening star-shaped, often in pairs in early spring. *T. clusiana* (lady tulip) is 10–12in

(25–30cm) tall with slender 1½in(4cm) flowers in mid-spring opening starry, coloured white and banded red on the outside; *T. c. chrysantha* is slightly less hardy with larger yellow flowers banded red.

Species tulips (continued)

T. fosterana is 1ft(30cm) tall with large scarlet, yellow-edged flowers, centred black and opening flat in mid-spring. *T. greigii* is 10–12in (25–30cm) tall, having grey-green leaves striped or mottled purple-brown or bronze, and 3in(8cm) orange-scarlet, yellow-edged flowers in early spring. *T. kaufmanniana* (water-lily tulip) is 6–10in(15–25cm) tall with 3in(8cm) white to creamy-yellow flowers in early spring, marked yellow and red in their centre. *T. marjoletti* is up to 2ft(60cm) tall with 1½–2in (4–5cm) flowers in very late spring. *T. praestans* is 10–12in (25–30cm) tall having ribbed leaves and small clusters of 2in(5cm) brick-red flowers in early spring; variety 'Fusilier' has flame-scarlet flowers. *T. pulchella* is dwarf, to 4–6in (10–15cm) in height with 1¼in (3cm) crimson to purple

Species tulips (continued)

flowers in very early spring in small clusters and each centred with a white-edged bluish patch; variety 'Violacea' has yellow-centred purple-violet flowers. *T. tarda* ILLUS LEFT p 114 (*T. dasystemon*) is dwarf, to 4–6in (10–15cm) tall with rosette leaves and 2in(5cm) starry flowers in early- to mid-spring, often several to a stem. *T. turkestanica* ILLUS RIGHT p 114 is 8–10in(20–25cm) tall with clusters of 1¼in(3cm) flowers in early spring. **Cult, P, D & D:** generally as for garden tulips (see p 119), but plant bulbs only 3–4in(8–10cm) deep.

Garden tulips

Very hardy hybrids derived
from various tulip species,
including several of those
listed on pp 112–114, long
valued for their bold colours
and flower shapes. Flowers,
unless stated, are held singly
on upright stalks and have six
petals opening cup- or goblet-
shaped in spring (flower sizes
quoted below are length ×
diameter). Leaves are generally quite broad and lance-
shaped, often with a greyish or
bluish tinge. Plants are
excellent for bedding and for
containers; all but the
shortest varieties are good
for cutting. Hybrids are
classified into 14 divisions
(recently revised) according to
flower form, season and
parentage; some 4,000
varieties are registered, a
selection of which are listed
below. **Spp & Vars:** SINGLE
EARLY – Plants are 10–24in
(25–60cm) tall with 3–4 × 3in
(8–10 × 8cm) cup-shaped
flowers in early- to mid-
spring, sometimes opening
flat in sunshine; varieties

include 'Apricot Beauty'
(apricot-pink tinged red),
'Bellona' (golden-yellow),
'General de Wet' (golden-
orange stippled scarlet),
'Keizerskroon' (red, edged
yellow) and 'Van der Neer'
(violet-purple). DOUBLE

Garden tulips (continued)

EARLY – Plants are 10–16in (25–40cm) tall with 2½–3 × 4in (6–8 × 10cm) long-lasting double paeony-like flowers in early- to mid-spring, opening wide in sun; varieties are 'Carlton' (deep red), 'Electra' (cherry red), 'Orange Nassau' (orange-red shaded mahogany) and 'Peach Blossom' (rose-pink). TRIUMPH – Plants are 16–20in(40–50cm) tall with 3–4 × 2–3in(8–10 × 5–8cm) conical flowers on sturdy stems in mid- to late spring, opening more rounded in sun and generally quite weather-resistant; varieties include 'Athleet' (white), 'Attila' ILLUS BELOW p 115, 'Garden Party' ILLUS ABOVE p115, and 'Kees Nelis' ('Ringo'; blood-red edged yellow). DARWIN HYBRIDS – Plants are 22–28in(55–70cm) tall with very large cupped flowers, up to 5 × 6–8in (12 × 15–20cm), in brilliant colours on strong stems in mid- to late spring; they are excellent for focal planting; varieties include 'Apeldoorn'

ILLUS p 116, 'Elizabeth Arden' (deep salmon, tinted violet), 'Golden Apeldoorn' (yellow) and 'Holland's Glorie' (very large soft orange-scarlet flowers). SINGLE LATE – Plants are generally 1½–2½ft(45–75cm) tall with variable but often large-cupped, squarish or oval flowers to 4–5 × 3–4in

Garden tulips (continued)

(10–12 × 8–10cm), often with
pointed petals, in late spring
to very early summer;
varieties include 'Clara Butt'
(salmon-rose), 'Golden
Harvest' (yellow), 'Queen of
Night' ILLUS ABOVE p 117, and
'Sorbet' (cream, flecked red);
Bouquet varieties with
several flowers per stem
include 'Orange Bouquet'
(vivid red-orange; yellow
base). LILY-FLOWERED –
Elegant and graceful plants
to 1½–2ft(45–60cm) tall with
narrow-waisted 3½–5 × 3in
(9–12 × 8cm) flowers with
pointed petals, in late spring
(best in sheltered spots);
varieties are 'China Pink'
(rose-pink), 'West Point'
(primrose-yellow) and 'White
Triumphator' (white).
FRINGED – Similar to Single
Late, but petals are edged
with crystal-shaped fringes;
mostly sold as mixtures
(sometimes as 'Orchid-
flowered'). VIRIDIFLORA –
Plants are mostly 10–12in
(25–30cm) tall, otherwise
similar to Single Late, but

Garden tulips (continued)

petals are partly greenish; varieties include 'Greenland' ILLUS BELOW p 117 (taller). REMBRANDT – Similar to Single Late, but colours are 'broken' into striped or feathered patterns; varieties include 'Absalon' ILLUS ABOVE p 118. PARROT – Plants are up to 20–26in(50–65cm) tall and similar to Single Late, but the long-lasting flowers are up to 5in(12cm) wide with frilly-edged, fringed and often twisted petals; varieties are 'Blue Parrot' (violet), 'Fantasy' (pink, often streaked green) and 'Texas Gold' (yellow, edged red). DOUBLE LATE – Sometimes called Paeony-Flowered, plants are 16–24in(40–60cm) tall with squat 3–4 × 4–5in(8–10 × 10–12cm) double flowers in mid- to late spring; varieties include 'Gold Medal' (yellow) and 'Mount Tacoma' ILLUS BELOW p 118. KAUFMANNIANA HYBRIDS – Also known as water-lily tulips, plants are 4–10in(10–25cm) tall with starry water-lily-like flowers

Garden tulips (continued)

opening flat to 2½in(6cm)
across and generally bi-
coloured in early spring;
many have striped or mottled
leaves; varieties include
'Shakespeare' (carmine-red
edged salmon, flushed scarlet
and centred yellow inside).
Fosterana hybrids – Plants
are generally 1–1½ft(30–45cm)
tall with large vivid flowers to
6 × 7–8in(15 × 18–20cm) in
early- to mid-spring;
varieties include 'Red
Emperor' illus p 119. Greigii
hybrids – Plants are 8–16in
(20–40cm) tall with wavy
leaves generally striped or
mottled with purple or brown,
and large vivid flowers to
4–5 × 4½in(10–12 × 13cm) in
mid- to late spring; dwarf
varieties include 'Plaisir'
(creamy-white, striped red)
and 'Red Riding Hood' (red;
black base). **Cult:** preferably
rich, well-drained soil in sun;
plant bulbs 5–6in(12–15cm)
deep in mid-autumn to early
winter (in warm climates bulbs
need eight weeks storage at
39–45°F[4–7°C] before

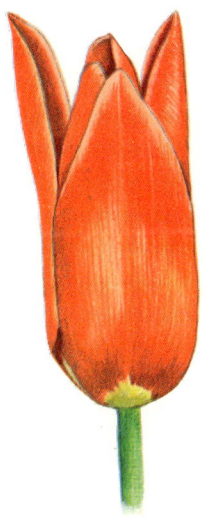

planting). Dead-head. Bulbs
are best lifted when the
foliage dies, dried and stored
until autumn. **P, D & D:** prone
to fire disease (protect bulbs
with fungicide).

Scarborough lily

A single species of tender South African bulb suitable for growing outdoors in frost-free areas or elsewhere making a good pot or container plant which can be moved under protection over winter. Plants are up to 2ft(60cm) tall with clusters of about ten funnel-shaped vermilion-red 3in(8cm) wide flowers in summer and early autumn. Leaves are bright, glossy and strap-shaped, and evergreen. **Spp & Vars:** *V. speciosa* (*V. purpurea*) is sometimes listed as *Amaryllis purpurea*. **Cult:** moist, fertile soil in full sun outdoors where hardy, or a proprietary potting compost in containers; plant bulbs shallowly with the tip exposed in early autumn. Keep moist throughout the year. **P, D & D:** generally none.

Zantedeschias

Generally tender to semi-hardy rhizomatous South African plants of the arum family with arrow-shaped and rather leathery leaves, and large funnel-shaped floral spathes (a flower-like structure surrounding a less significant fleshy spike, the spadix, of true flowers). Plants are generally 2–3ft(60–90cm) tall and best grown in large pots and taken indoors in winter. **Spp & Vars:** *Z. aethiopica* (common arum/ calla lily) is semi- to moderately hardy with white spathes to 10in(25cm) long and is best standing in water; variety 'Crowborough' is moderately hardy. *Z. elliottiana* ILLUS has bright yellow spathes and spotted leaves. **Cult:** moist, humus-rich soil in sun or partial shade; plant rhizomes 2–3in(5–8cm) deep in autumn. **P, D & D:** generally none, but may rot in cold and wet conditions.

Zephyr lilies, flowers of the west wind

Rather crocus-like bulbs with trumpet-shaped flowers opening starry, and grassy leaves. **Spp & Vars:** *Z. candida* ILLUS BELOW LEFT is moderately hardy, to 4–8in (10–20cm) tall with white, sometimes pink-tinged, 1½in (4cm) flowers in early autumn. *Z. rosea* ILLUS BELOW RIGHT is semi-hardy, to 1ft(30cm) tall, flowering in summer and best grown under glass except where summers are very warm. **Cult:** moist, but well-drained soil in warm sun; plant 4in(10cm) deep in spring. Mulch in winter where hardy, otherwise lift and store over winter in damp peat. **P, D & D:** generally none.

Index